AN AUDIT TENDER:
A True Journey Of Discovery

Graham Hall

Published in Great Britain by
L.R. Price Publications Ltd, 2021
27 Old Gloucester Street,
London, WC1N 3AX
www.lrpricepublications.com

ISBN-13: 9781838339562

I dedicate this book to my wife and family. Your support and participation in editing, reviewing and challenging me was truly awesome.

Contents

Foreword

The journey of an audit tender process is one of learning and adapting as the journey of discovery unfolds.

In writing this book I do not claim to be an expert. Indeed, my own journey has been one of starting with a blank page, albeit with a clear mandate as to the end game and then filling in the gaps as the journey unfolded.

This journey related to defining and managing an audit tender process for one of the largest FMCG companies in the world. The audit RFP covered both the audit of the parent company and the 430 statutory audits of the group.

Auditor rotation for "Public Interest Entities" (PIEs) is now mandatory for European entities (requiring them to rotate their audit providers every twelve years); the jury is still out on the question on whether other non-EU countries will follow this approach.

In my own case, the company was listed outside the EU, but the Group Audit Committee, supported by the Board, decided that for good governance purposes and given the significant years since it last looked outside for its external audit providers, now was the time.

When I was asked to prepare papers outlining a high-level overview of an audit tender process, including designing the process and the relevant touch points in the business likely to be impacted, I reached to the internet for guidance.

After countless hours of trawling the net for hints, I came away largely empty handed and looking for inspiration.

So, I leave it up to you, the reader, to decide if I found inspiration or I went up a blind alley towards confusion and a multitude of ill-defined guidelines, un-actionable and incapable of delivering a fair, balanced and transparent tender process.

EU Auditor Rotation Regulations

- Mandatory Audit Firm rotation for all Public Interest Entities (Credit institutions, Insurance companies, companies that have securities listed on a regulated market)
- Maximum duration of audit engagement may not exceed 10 years (unless a Member State decides to extend rotation period of maximum 20 years in the case of tendering)
- 4 year cooling off period after the end of the statutory audit services before the audit firm can be reappointed.
- PIE to perform a transparent audit tendering process with close involvement of audit Committee
- Increased restrictions on Non audit Services provided to PIEs.
- Audit committee independence and technical competence to be reinforced.
- Extension of the functions assigned to the Audit Committee.
- Cooperation between national audit oversight bodies will be strengthened at EU level through establishment of the Committee of European Auditing Oversight Bodies

Transition arrangements

- Depends on the number of years the audit firm has been in place at the date of entry into force (16.06.2014)
- If the audit firm was in place for more than 20 years: by 2020
- If the audit firm was in place between 11 and 20 years: 2023
- At the latest by 2024
- Each Member state could impose stricter rules

M   Rotation Requirements

In the pages which follow, I have the stated aim of giving the reader an insight into what I learnt, how I learnt it and how I put this into practice. Maybe, just maybe, you will find my journey resonates with your path and just maybe helps you navigate towards the destination you have been set.

Defining a process

The decision to commence an audit tender process and accompanying RFP is clearly an emotive subject, with management and non-executive boards often conflicted between operational and pure governance issues.

A multitude of opinions will ultimately drive the decision to tender the preferred audit provider.

Once made, it is key that the consensus is galvanized towards a common objective and through this ensure full alignment in defining both the process to be followed and, more importantly, the key success factors which will drive the ultimate decision.

The decision to tender is, of course, a decisive one and indicative of management and a company's board's openness to expose the business to a new regime of oversight and governance.

Management and the Board need to be aligned on the "why and how" but also, more importantly, on a joint vision of what the future audit environment should constitute.

Key factors that cannot be ignored are the audit environment, whether the company is in a period of change, whether this impacts on the risk environment, whether the business is confident of its control and resultant risk relative to its financial statements.

Having made the decision to launch a tender process and accompanying RFP and in advance of inviting firms to participate, a detailed outline of the anticipated process should be prepared.

In preparing this, a Project Manager should be appointed. Key to this appointment is their knowledge and understanding of, and familiarity with the entire business, both its footprint and the key market's associated risk drivers.

Fundamental to the process is ensuring all stakeholders are briefed and engaged in the process. This should include full integration of the stakeholders to the selection process, such that all the organization is seen as key contributors to the final choice of audit providers.

Preparation is key and should **NOT** be underestimated.

Success Factors

In starting the audit tender process the Project Manager should reach out to key stakeholders (Board, Audit Committee and Senior Management) in order to define the success factors which will influence their final appointment. This should be based on a simple questionnaire with basic scoring as below:

Questionnaire to Senior Management re Audit Expectations

Following the instruction from the AC to prepare for a Tender of the Group Preferred Audit provider, we now seek a short input from yourself in order to ensure the tender is targeted to the correct scope and expectation of Senior Management.

It would greatly assist to this thought process if you could indicate below what would be your priorities in selecting the preferred audit firm.

To this end could I ask that you complete the following 12 questions, indicating the importance you place on each point with scores of 1 to 10 (1=low importance, 10= high importance)

1. Total cost to Audit

2. Ensure compliance at minimal cost within Regulatory Requirements

3. Audit materiality levels set to support strong Nestle Internal compliance culture at optimal cost

4. Demonstrably strong compliance mindset

5. Reputation of the tendering firm

6. Business sector knowledge and experience providing insight into industry practices

7. Commercially aware and insightful lead partner

8. Proactivity in identifying saving/efficiency opportunities

9. Leveraging of technologies as part of the Audit process

10. Insight from local audit teams covering risk and local Compliance

11. Acceptance of Nestle accounting methodology and basis of Assumptions for valuation (IMPA, PPA etc.)

12. Open feedback ensuring forward looking risk identification

Selection Criteria

MHC Group Audit Tender Selection Criteria

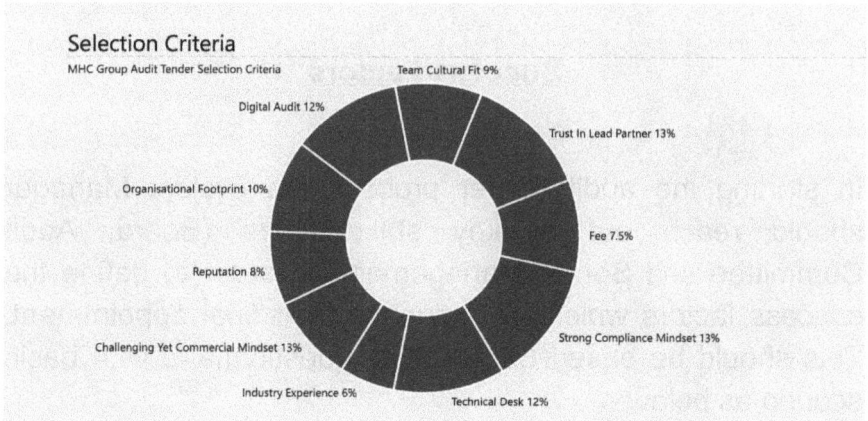

- Team Cultural Fit 9%
- Digital Audit 12%
- Trust In Lead Partner 13%
- Organisational Footprint 10%
- Fee 7.5%
- Reputation 8%
- Strong Compliance Mindset 13%
- Challenging Yet Commercial Mindset 13%
- Industry Experience 6%
- Technical Desk 12%

M   Audit Tender Graphs

4

The above chart should be included in the audit firm briefing and will be one of the most important elements to be shared in order to provide the framework within which the firms will build their proposal. Worthy of consideration, in addition to these success factors, is to reach out to the wider finance community for their input on what matters to them.

At the end of the day, it is these members of the wider finance community who will work with the appointed firm in future audits. It is therefore appropriate to take full account of their perspective of operational concerns surrounding the audit.

In my case I sought feedback from a wide cross section of the finance community across the world to identify "what matters" to them and how the client/auditor relationship could bring true added value to them on the frontline.

The chart below was then shared with all participants to the tender at the outset along with the success factors; this enables the firm to refine the selection of their teams and ensure that they understand what the front line expects.

Project Tender
Success Factors/what matters to MHC
Approach to Audit Quality
The proposal should outline an audit approach that is based on obtaining an understanding of MHC's activities, operating systems, personnel and specific needs, whilst also being tailored to both the size and complexity of MHC
Audit materiality levels should be set to support the strong MHC Internal Compliance culture at an optimal cost
The audit approach will need to be mindful of the changing environment across the MHC Group with the move of significant Accounting and Reporting activities to both internal and external shared service centers
The proposed Reporting Units to be included in the scope of the Group Audit in support of the publication of the Group's Financial Statements should be enough to address the MHC risk profile
The audit firm's organization and locations of its offices and personnel need to be enough to ensure a smooth

and efficient delivery of the defined audit scope within the timetable provided

Team Knowledge and Experience
The proposed Lead Partner should demonstrate a collaborative yet independent mindset, with a strong understanding of MHC, its goals and aspirations, whilst also showing strong leadership skills, being able to articulate a position with strength and clarity
The Partner should demonstrate an empathy with MHC management such that a sound collaborative working relationship can be built over time, enabling mutual respect within the boundaries of an auditor/client relationship
The tender proposal should specify the strengths of the assigned team members as well as their years of experience in the industry and type of engagement the MHC represents
The proposal needs to highlight the audit firm's commitment to professional training and staff continuity in line with our requirement of a maximum of 1/3 of the team rotating each year
The tender proposal should provide the audit firm's background, client base and the competencies of its Technical Desk
The audit firm should demonstrate its personnel are familiar with MHC's business in relation to our size, locations and strategic business goals

Data Analytics
The proposal must demonstrate a strong understanding of data analytics as a key component of an effective audit, whilst also showing a desire to place significant reliance on centralized data analytics as a driver towards efficiency of the audit process
Value-Added Services
The proposal should provide a listing of additional value-added services the firm provides beyond the audit engagement (e.g. proactively monitor and communicate topics relevant to our financial and business operations all year long that may impact on our future success)

Scope and Pricing of the Engagement

The tender proposal must clearly provide a framework for the scope, timing and resources required to complete the audit engagement

The Tender proposal should specify the price for the audit of MHC, split by reporting unit, how it will be billed, the payment terms and outlining how the fees will evolve over time, given the targeted efficiency savings outlined in the proposal

The proposal needs to address all items requested by MHC, whether verbally or in the RFO/Tender Briefing

The proposal should provide the expected Audit Fees relative to the Statutory Audits of all entities of the Group required to prepare audited financial statements

The proposal should address the question of independence, being mindful of any apparent conflicts of interest represented by an appointment of the firm as our Auditor and how you would propose to address these

The proposed fee should be competitive being based on a solid understanding of the global footprint of MHC and the experience the audit firm would bring to the engagement

Target audience and invites to participate
in the tender process

The choice of target firms to be invited to participate in the RFP will often be driven by the size, footprint and complexity of the company.

Big is not necessarily beautiful but may still be the only practical solution.

Factors relevant to the choice of participant firms are likely to be, amongst others, locations of local offices, relevant experience in the company's industry and reputation of the firm.

Inevitably, members of the audit committee and internal management will have opinions of the "best fit" firm, often based on their previous experience of working with them.

In some cases, the current incumbent may be precluded from participating in the tender owing to regulatory rotation restrictions. However, regardless of the size and footprint of the company the decision to tender the audit must demonstrate the company's strong governance mindset.

Owing to recent legislation, many company boards are faced with the need to put their audit out to tender; indeed, even in jurisdictions where there is no requirement to tender, investor pressure is focusing management towards this need.

The decision to tender an audit is a complex and troubling one for many companies, often due to the high level of change in the organization where the idea of a change in auditor adds further to the stress already faced by many companies.

During my own experience of this decision process, I often heard management exchange counter views, for example, "We are going through so much change as an organization; this is not the time to be contemplating a change in auditor." Conversely, "It is because we are going through so much change that now is the time to change auditor."

Of even greater importance is that having made the decision to tender and chosen those firms you want to participate, all firms are considered equal and are treated as such.

In terms of how many firms should be invited to participate there is no quick answer; this ultimately is a question of balance and a desire to build a competitive process.

In my own case, the "big four" were all invited including the incumbent firm.

The invitation to participate in the tender should be addressed to the firm's Head of Audit in the country where the company's parent is located; this can be problematic as often when you go to the firm's website, email addresses are only visible if you raise a specific request.

In my case we wanted to maintain the confidentiality of our plan to tender. Fortunately, I managed to locate the required email addresses, although I was not certain of having achieved this until the firms' responses to our invite came in.

The invitation should include a date by which the firms are required to confirm their wish to participate in the tender along with a request to provide the contact details of the firm's representative who will coordinate communications until a Lead Partner is chosen by the firm to lead the pursuit.

At this point the firms should also be asked to sign a non-disclosure agreement (NDA) covering all representatives of the firm who would participate. The NDA is not an exhaustive document but is legally binding on each firm. An example of an NDA would be as follows:

NON-DISCLOSURE AGREEMENT

This non-disclosure agreement ("**Agreement**") is entered by and between:

1) **MHC SA** (which together with its subsidiaries and affiliates is herein referred to as the "**MHC Group**")

and

2) _____ (the "Auditor")

MHC Group and the Auditor are hereinafter each referred to as a "Party" and jointly as the "Parties". The Party disclosing information to the other Party pursuant to this Agreement shall hereinafter be referred to as the "**Disclosing Party**" and the party receiving information from the Disclosing Party shall be referred to as the "**Recipient**".

BACKGROUND

A) The Parties have entered discussions relating to a tender for external audit services regarding the MHC Group (the "Objective").

B) As part of the tender process, the Parties will exchange certain confidential information in accordance with the terms and conditions of this Agreement.

1 DEFINITION OF CONFIDENTIAL INFORMATION

In this Agreement, "Confidential Information" means any item of information, whether in written, digitalized or oral form, which is received by the Recipient or any directors, officers, employees, advisors, affiliates or subsidiaries

15

("Representatives") of the Recipient from the Disclosing Party or any Representatives of the Disclosing Party in relation to the Objective, with the exception of information that:

a)   is publicly known or will become a matter of general knowledge other than by breach of this Agreement,

b)   the Recipient can prove was in its possession before receiving it from the Disclosing Party, or

c)   the Recipient has received or will receive from a third party without restraints as to the disclosure thereof.

2   USE OF CONFIDENTIAL INFORMATION

The Recipient agrees and acknowledges that the Confidential Information may be used solely for the Objective and not for any other purpose.

3   DISCLOSURE RESTRICTIONS

3.1   The Confidential Information will be held in complete and strict confidence and may only be disclosed by the Recipient to its Representatives on a strict need-to-know-basis for the purpose of the Objective.

3.2   The Recipient undertakes to ensure that each of its Representatives who receives Confidential Information is made aware of and observes the obligations under this Agreement.

3.3   Section 3.1 above does not, however, apply to the extent that the Recipient is required to make a disclosure of Confidential Information by law or pursuant to any order of court or other competent authority, or, if a Party needs to use the Confidential Information in respect of any dispute between the

Parties, in which cases the Recipient shall inform the Disclosing Party in advance (to the extent not prohibited by law or regulation) and shall limit such disclosure of Confidential Information to the strict minimum required.

4 TERM

This Agreement shall enter into force when duly signed by both Parties and shall remain in force for a period of two years from the date of signing or, if earlier, until signing of an engagement letter for external audit services regarding the MHC Group, except for information kept pursuant to sec. 5.2 hereafter, in which case the obligations under this Agreement shall remain in full force and effect in relation to information so kept.

5 RETURN OF CONFIDENTIAL INFORMATION

5.1 Upon written request by the Disclosing Party, the Recipient agrees that it will return or destroy (at the Disclosing Party's discretion) all written or digitalized copies of any document in the Recipient's (including any Representative's) possession, containing Confidential Information.

5.2 This does not apply to information that the Recipient is required to keep according to any law or regulation nor to information kept for the purpose of ensuring compliance with the Recipient's obligations herein; in such cases information to be kept shall be limited to the strict minimum required.

6 GOVERNING LAW AND JURISDICTION

This Agreement shall be governed by and construed in accordance with the laws of Switzerland without regard to its principles of conflict of laws.

This Agreement has been duly executed in two (2) original copies, of which each of the Parties has taken one copy.

Date: _____

_____

MHC SA

Date: _____

_____

[AUDITOR'S COMPANY NAME]

The governance of the tender process should be respected by all sides; this means all interaction between representatives of both the company and the firms needs to be carefully managed by the Project Manager (PM).

To this end, all meetings regarding the tender should be attended by the PM. It should be made clear to all personnel of the company and the tendering firms that this protocol absolutely precludes side-bar discussions in order to ensure delivery of a fair and balanced tender process.

Many elements of a company's finance community will have previously had and likely still do have, an ongoing relationship with the firms due to interactions linked to assignments outside the audit provision.

Whilst these need to be continued, such interactions must not be allowed to stray into the area of the audit tender. It is human nature for the firms to use every possible link into the company to try to gain a competitive advantage but this needs to be curtailed.

The behaviour of each firm in respecting the protocols you set for the tender is perhaps indicative of that firm's own internal culture.

This principal and the associated protocols need to be communicated and enforced at the highest level in the organizations of both the company and the participating firms.

Briefing of firms and tender preparation

Ensuring all key stakeholders are fully briefed and able to be supportive of the tender process is key and will underpin the delivery of a comprehensive, fair and balanced process.

In preparing a detailed briefing for the firms it is important to provide enough detail, such that all firms regardless of their familiarity with the company are brought to the same level of understanding of the organization, as well as how information will be shared during the process.

The level of familiarity is a key consideration given the stated aim of running a fair and balanced tender. Clearly where the incumbent firm is also participating, they will have several years of knowledge, not inherently available to the other firms.

The tender briefing provided to all firms is the first step in ensuring you provide the required balanced landscape. The briefing you provide to the firms should be comprehensive whilst leaving the detail to be found in your data room.

The intent is to explain the process that will be followed including a high-level process timeline, along with due notice of the meetings and visits that are envisaged with senior management, functional heads and key markets.

In order to demonstrate the size of the audit engagement a full list of reporting units along with their respective net sales, operating profit and invested capital (by unit/entity) should be included.

It should also be worth considering whether the incumbent's current scope of units forming the audit scope for the Group should be disclosed, or whether you invite each firm to define its proposed scope as part of the process. Such an approach leaves it to the tendering firms to define it based on their own assessment of risk, materiality and their own assessment and understanding of the company's control environment.

Additionally, a full listing of legal entities requiring statutory or regulatory audits should be included.

Whilst it is for a company's management to define the content of the initial briefing, you may find the following a helpful guide, based on my own experience and feedback I received following the briefing I provided:

i) **Introduction** A short note thanking the firms for their participation and commitment including a comment on the process and governance along with a statement of intent with regard to the company's intent of running a fair, balanced and transparent process.

M
MARC HALL
CONSULTING

Introduction

MHC is delighted that your firm has accepted our invitation to participate in the Tender process for Preferred Audit Provider to the MHC Group.

It is fundamental to MHC that the tender process is both balanced and fair to all participants whilst also being transparent to all.

We appreciate the effort and commitment that will be required by your firm in meeting the timelines of the process. We would assure you of our equal commitment to facilitate and support all interactions with MHC such that you are able to prepare an informed Tender.

During the Tender process there will be opportunities for your proposed Lead Partner to meet with Senior Management, dates of these meetings will be communicated in the coming weeks.

In the following document, we aim to provide all firms with a detailed briefing of our expectations of the process, including outline visit plans to key markets and the agendas applicable to these.

This briefing document also includes our view of the success criteria that will drive our decision as well as an insight as to what is key to the MHC Family with regards to its Audit provider.

MHC is currently in a period of change, its E2E initiative will see significant activities moving above market over the coming years, during the Tender process we will aim to provide all firms with a sound understanding of the future landscape.

MHC looks forward to working with you during the Tender Process in an open and collaborative manner.

We hope the Tender Project deliverable will live up to the high standards we set ourselves in MHC and meet your expectations at the same time.

ii) **Audit and reporting process** This is a key section and sets the expectation and timelines of the tender process. Within this section there should also be reference to the areas considered as fundamental drivers of the decision and you believe each firm has an opportunity to differentiate themselves, for example, data analytics and audit automation, scope and fees for the group audit and any key expectations of the audit process.

Some firms have also developed tools to support the audit process which facilitate sharing of information and PBC documents without the inherent security risk of sending documents via email.

In this section the company's expectations around timing and content of the written tender proposal as well as the presentation to the selection panel should be outlined.

The below document was provided to each firm within the briefing document I prepared:

Audit and Reporting Process

The successful tender for the MHC group audit will envisage delivery of a continuous audit process, wherein findings will be raised and addressed in real time during the financial year.

Data Analytics

It is envisaged the auditor will place significant reliance on Central Data Analytics, both in relation to the Group scope audit as well as for the Statutory Audit cycle for those markets not in scope for Group purposes.

MHC has developed its own range of Data Analytics scripts which will be available to the audit firm to support its extraction requirements. The reliance on Central Data Analytics is expected to provide cost-efficient audits with ongoing delivery of fee reductions.

Timelines

MHC ordinarily receives the reporting from its markets on workday 10 each quarter; a review process follows such that final consolidated financial statements are available by workday 20.

MHC currently publishes sales and the sales metrics on a quarterly basis, half-yearly. It also reports its full performance metrics in a condensed format. Typically, half-year results are published during the last week of July whilst the full year financial statements are published in mid-February.

MHC will require an audit/review process to be implemented such that the Group is able to publish its Financial Statements for H1 supported by an auditor review during week 30 and fully audited Annual Financial Statements during week 7.

Prior to the half-year and full year publication, a full mock-up of the financial statements to be published is shared with the audit team to ensure full alignment on our planned notes and disclosures.

Fees and Scope

The fee is expected to be comprehensive in nature and include provision for reasonable scope changes.

The tender submission is expected to provide for an itemized fee both by Reporting Unit for the Group scope audit and by Entity for the Statutory scope audits.

The tender will be split between the Group Audit scope including the sign off of the Group published Financial Statements at both the half-year (June) and the full year (December) including the Statutory reporting of those entities (NB. Half-year is limited to a review, with no opinion required) and the Statutory Audits of all markets not forming part of the Group audit scope.

The tendering firms are invited to define which reporting units they would require to include in the scope of works for the Audit Opinion of MHC Group Financial Statements.

The tendering firms will also be open to define the Group and Component materiality within which their opinion will be framed.

Audit Process

A "buddy system" has evolved during the last three years wherein each member of the Market Reporting Team in FC-FRA has direct and regular interaction with a lead member of the Central Audit Team. These buddies are allocated specific markets/businesses and the interactions are used to ensure timely and proactive action should audit issues arise during the year.

A key component of the audit process is to provide for regular interaction between the Lead Partner on the Global assignment and key F&C personnel.

We would ask that you define how you would propose to ensure you are kept fully aware of the business, its evolution and decisions of management that would have potential to influence your audit process or ultimate opinion.

Deliverables of Tender Submission

All tendering firms will be required to submit a written proposal by 15th May 2019. **Appendix X** lists MHC expectation of what this document should include. Firms are free to expand on this as they deem appropriate whilst MHC would request you are mindful of the volume of information you would ask the selection panel to digest.

Presentation to the MHC Selection Panel

These are scheduled for week of xxx, two-hour time slots to be communicated in the coming weeks.

Firms are free to define the vehicle to be used for the presentations (power point, electronic interactive format, iPad, etc.)

The tender presentations should be mindful of the allotted time (2 hours) and allow for enough time for Q&A.

All firms are free to define the content to be included but should clearly demonstrate a link to the previously submitted written tender, focusing on salient points you would like to emphasize to the selection panel.

Below is a list of items we believe would be beneficial.

1. Overview of Firm

2. Global organization (including footprint and geographic coverage)

3. Resourcing and experience of your team

4. Introduction of the proposed Lead Partner

5. Introduction of key members of the central team

6. Industry experience and client base

7. Proposed scope of works (including identifying RU to be in scope) in delivery of the Audited Financial Statements of MHC SA

8. Total Fee proposal for the Audit of Financial Statements of MHC SA and the statutory audits of those markets included in the scope defined above.

9.   Total Fee proposal for the statutory audits of all remaining Legal entities requiring audit

10.   How the firm leverages Data Analytics in its audit methodology and how you will aim to utilize this in delivery of ongoing cost savings

11.   Areas you believe you can add value to MHC

12.   Your understanding of MHC Risk profile

13.   Explore any potential conflict of interest that should be considered (Partner or Senior Management engaged in Audit or Non-Audit work for an MHC competitor)

iii)   **Legal and regulatory environment** This section enables the company to outline the statutory framework, applicable accounting and auditing in the parent company's home country. It is also intended to outline the accounting principles applicable to the Group's reporting.

iv) **Schedule of deliverables to be included in the tender submission** This section of the briefing should be highly prescriptive of what management expect to see in the written proposal. In some instances, the company may choose to place a limit on the length of the proposal. In my case we specifically left this to the discretion of each firm, albeit with the caveat that the density of the proposal would be indicative of the quality of each firm's communication prowess and their ability to provide focused and on point messages.

Key points to be covered should be identified here, along with clear guidance as to expected content for each point. Whilst not exhaustive, it sets out the minimum whilst still allowing each firm to add additional content which they feel will differentiate them in the process.

Below is the schedule of deliverables I included in the briefing I prepared:

Schedule of deliverables to be included in tender submission

Deliverables of Tender Submission

All tendering firms will be required to submit a written proposal by 15th May 2019 encompassing the following information:

(Whilst we do not seek to limit the length of your written proposal, it should reflect the quality of your firm's communication and be focused and to the point. We would also appreciate if it was prefixed with an Executive Summary.)

Written Tender Submission

Schedule of deliverables to be included in tender submission

The tender document should include the following information:

Details of your firm

▪A statement summarising the benefits to MHC SA of selecting your firm

▪The organization and structure of the firm, as it is relevant to this engagement inclusive of Partners and Management

▪Industry experience and client base

Resourcing

Name and CV of the proposed Lead Audit Partner. MHC will require the opportunity for both the Group CFO and the Head of FRA to interview the proposed candidate.

Names of your core service team, location and

relevant experience

Personal fit with the management team and culture

The time the key team members will commit to this appointment

Succession planning and steps to be taken in order to ensure staff continuity. Note that MHC would expect a maximum rotation of those management and staff assigned to the Group Audit to be no greater than one third per annum.

Approach

Understanding of our broader business needs and risks

Proposed scope of Reporting Units to be included in the Group Audit in order to provide an opinion of the MHC Group Financial Statements

The tendering firms are open to define the Group and Component materiality within which their opinion will be framed.

Processes for delivering audit services, which are customized, proactive and aligned with MHC's specific needs

Processes that your firm will employ to address matters related to client satisfaction, performance measurement and continuous improvement

How you will liaise and work with our internal audit and areas where you envisage placing reliance on their activities

Demonstrate how you will use Centralized Data

Analytics to deliver your service with MHC system data and an overview of your firm's current experience utilising data analytics, inclusive of measures you would apply to ensure MHC internal access security protocols are not compromised

How you will report your audit findings to us

Audit Transition (if applicable)

Process for audit transition and the newly appointed firm's proposal to transition out of non-audit service provision where relevant

Relevant previous experience with audit transitions of similar companies

Transition plan such that the newly appointed firm can commence the review of the financial statements for the six months to 30th June 2020 and the audit of the financial statements for the year ended 31st December 2020

Quality assurance

Describe the internal processes used for quality assurance

Describe your firm's approach to resolving accounting and financial reporting issues

Independence and governance

Internal practices to ensure compliance with independence requirements and freedom from conflicts of interest

Summary of relationships that may reasonably be thought to bear on independence and the proposed plan to manage them (e.g. non-audit services)

Details of current audit assignments of the tendering firm with regard to companies likely to be competitors to the MHC Group

Confirmation by your firm that it will take all necessary steps to ensure its independence

Fees

Competitive fee quote to complete the global audit for year ending 31st December 2020 inclusive of the half-year review requirements

Proposed scope of markets (Reporting units "RU") to be included in the scope of works for delivery of audited Financial Statements of MHC SA

Fee proposal by RU for the audit of the financial statements of MHC SA and the statutory audits of the component legal entities

Fee proposal by legal entity for the statutory audits of all remaining entities requiring audited financial statements not included within the Group scope audit

The basis on which fees will be determined in future years inclusive of meeting efficiency gains able to deliver year on year savings over the coming years

General overview of the schedule and timing of billings

The fee is expected to be comprehensive in nature and include provision for reasonable scope changes.

General

At present the Group Audit provider works with the MHC local teams to provide ongoing training and support on developments in IFRS and associated fiscal accounting and reporting requirements; these are not a contributor to additional audit fees.

MHC will require open access to the Swiss Audit Partner and his/her team and the Swiss Technical Desk in order to maintain strong two-way dialogue on issues with the potential to impact the Group Reporting.

Outline your proposed audit approach to non-financial disclosures including our sustainability statement.

v)   **High-level timelines** By sharing at the outset of the process the high-level timelines to be followed in the process, the firms are made aware of the preparation activities with associated touch points and meetings that are planned for the formal element of the process. Never lose sight of the fact that key personnel from each firm will be engaged in the tender. These people are often senior members of the firm and will be actively engaged in existing audit assignments which you should expect to take priority. As such sharing of the timetable provides them with adequate opportunity to balance their agendas.

vi) **Governance** Governance surrounding all participants (internal and external) is essential if the tender process is to deliver in line with its stated objectives. The document below was included in our briefing in order to set the bar on Governance at the appropriate level:

Governance

The Audit Tender process is a highly confidential and emotive subject. For this to be successful, it will require that we adopt a transparent open approach to all tendering firms, being respectful of the significant investment in terms of time and effort they will put behind their tender.

MHC will share significant previously undisclosed information to a wide community of external participants from the tendering firms; to this end all tendering firms will also be required to sign individual NDAs.

With regard to the MHC internal community, those acting on the project team and those identified as "key contributors" as well as all members of the management community who will have cause to interact with the tendering firms will need to follow strict protocols.

These protocols are intended to ensure all participating firms have access to the same level of information and that MHC are also seen to be ensuring access to key decision makers that is balanced and fair on all tendering firms.

All members of the project team and the key contributors will be required to respect the protocol of confidentiality; this would inherently mean that no information, documentation or anecdotal information of which they have become aware during the project may be shared outside the project team.

Similarly, during any interaction that project team members may have with participating firms during the process, it is essential they remain mindful of the need for a balanced tender process and as such not to share any information not widely available to the other tendering firms, which could place a firm in a position of advantage.

All market visits, dialogue with the management community as well as members of the Audit Committee will be coordinated by the project manager (PM), thus ensuring all firms are acting on a balanced "playing field" with commensurate levels of access to decision makers within MHC.

Where a tendering firm asks for specific non-planned access to management, this will be coordinated by the PM with similar access being afforded to the other firms, should they wish to avail themselves of the opportunity.

In addition to this internal protocol, all tendering firms will be expected to respect the process and communication channels.

To this end, except as communicated and planned by the PM, members of the tendering firms (both regarding the central tender team and that firm's local representation) should have no unplanned direct interaction with MHC personnel. This will ensure no competitive advantage is perceived from these interactions.

All tendering firms and MHC personnel are bound by Non-Disclosure Agreements; under no circumstances should any party (both MHC and the Tendering Firms) hold "side-bar" discussions unless authorized specifically by the MHC Project Manager (Graham Hall).

To this end, any and all discussions between MHC personnel or its representatives and the tendering firms must be agreed by the Project Manager.

A market visit agenda will be provided to all tendering firms. This will outline the dates available for each market to be visited; it will then be for the tendering firms to elect which markets they wish to visit. The PM will coordinate and attend all visits and ensure these are conducted in a timely fashion with each firm being afforded a full day or part thereof each for their visit.

Obviously, the intent is to ensure each tendering firm is kept separate during market visits whilst at the same time not placing too high a disruption on local MHC management.

With regard to the need for absolute transparency and a balanced fair process, every effort will be made by MHC to deliver to this promise.

If any firm feels that information that they require is not forthcoming, or the process appears weighted towards another tendering firm, then such concerns should in the first instance be raised with the MHC Project Manager (Graham Hall).

Should the concerns continue, then the affected firm should contact Mr. Bryan (Head of FRA) to raise this concern.

vii) **Market Visit Planning** Providing an opportunity for the firms to get closer to the operations is fundamental in ensuring they can build an effective, comprehensive audit proposal. I will share later more detail regarding managing such visits and the agenda to follow; however, it is important to ensure top-down management support and engagement to the visits as they provide crucial insights to the business and the DNA of the company. The visits are also an opportunity for the firms to witness first-hand the control environment present in the company beyond that provided through your data room.

In defining those units to be part of your visit schedule, you should be mindful of the logistics challenge these may represent. Time zones and long flights can really sap the energy of the PM and the firm's personnel. It is also important to expose the firms to the material units as well as the locations where accounting and other back office functionality are performed, often in above market shared service sites.

viii) **Data room** As previously mentioned, it is essential to delivering a fair tender process, to ensure all participating firms are provided with enough information such that no one firm, including the incumbent, is disadvantaged by a lack of information leading to a lack of understanding of the business.

The data room should be comprehensive and available to all firms. As part of your briefing document, you should share an overview of the expected content of the data room; this also demonstrates that your company treats the process with a high degree of commitment. You should always be mindful that each firm will invest heavily in its participation in the tender, so being able to demonstrably show your company's commitment is key.

By providing this transparency well in advance of the formal commencement of the process and prior to the data room going live, the firms can better plan the resources and effort they will need to put in place. The choice of data room provider and the process to populate it is outlined in more detail later. However, below is the data room index provided within the briefing document; this clearly builds on the firm's expectations for the process:

			MHC Group Audit Tender Dataroom information requirements	Subject Expert	Moderator
Ref	Subject	Short description	Content		
1	Group structure				
1.1		Organisation	— Organisation chart, showing key individuals, responsibilities and reporting lines including Finance, Compliance, Corporate Audit, Commercial organization including clusters and categories, specialist areas (such as IT, Treasury, Tax, Enterprise support etc.)		
1.2		Locations	— Location of operations globally (offices, sales offices and factories/distribution centers including addresses and number of personnel		
1.3		JVs	— Overview of Joint Ventures (CPW, Franeri etc.) & Associates		
1.4		Auditor rotation	— Detail of Auditor Rotation requirements impacting the Group		
1.5	MHC Skin Health structure	NSH	— Business is subject to Strategic Review, as such it is excluded from the Tender Process until further notice		
1.6	XYZ Group structure				
1.61		Organisation	— Organisation chart, showing key individuals, responsibilities and reporting lines including Finance, Compliance, Commercial organization including clusters and categories, specialist areas (such as IT, Enterprise support etc.)		
1.62		Locations	— Location of operations globally (offices, sales offices and factories/distribution centers including addresses and number of personnel		
2	Key financial data				
2.1		LE vs Reporting Unit	— Group structure chart and how it compares to the structure in the financial reporting system (if different) GEMS to Magnitude		
2.2		Statutory Accounts	— Latest statutory accounts of entities requiring an audit for last 2 years (available via a link to the existing database)		
2.3		Statutory Accounts	— Breakdown by Legal Entity all entities requiring an audit (indication whether statutory, regulatory and group reporting fees)		
2.4		Audit Fees	— 2018/17 Audit Fees, Non-Audit and Consultancy fees by Reporting Unit		
2.5		Key figures	— Key figures by Reporting Unit (NN6, GM, OP1, OP2, OP3 Net Assets etc.)		
2.51		Key figures	— Consolidated view Inclusive of central entries and inter co eliminations		
2.52		Key figures	— Local package amount		
3	Financial results for the last 2 years				
3.1		Key figures	— Breakdowns of revenue and operating profit (before and after tax) by Reporting Unit		
3.2		Performance Matrices	— Explanation and calculation methodology of the four key factors (SCOM / SACT)		
3.3		Key figures	— Goodwill/intangible Assets by Reporting Unit		
3.4		Balance Sheet	— Balance Sheet by Reporting Unit		
3.41		Balance Sheet	— Consolidated view inclusive of central entries and inter co eliminations		
3.42		Balance Sheet	— Local package amount		
3.5	MHC Skin Health financial results for the last 2 years	NSH	— Business is subject to Strategic Review, as such it is excluded from the Tender Process until further notice		
3.6	MHC Group Financial results for the last 2 years				
3.61		Key figures	— Breakdowns of revenue and operating profit (before and after tax) by Reporting Unit		
3.62		Statutory Accounts	— 2018/17 Audit Fees, Non-Audit and Consultancy fees by Reporting Unit		
3.63		Balance Sheet	— Balance Sheet by Reporting Unit		
3.64		Key figures	— Key figures by Reporting Unit (NN6, GM, OP1, OP2, OP3 Net Assets etc.)		

				Subject Expert	Moderator
MHC Group Audit Tender Dataroom Information requirements					
Ref	**Subject**	**Short description**	**Content**		
1	**Group structure**				
1,1		Organisation	— Organization chart, showing key individuals, responsibilities and reporting lines including Finance, Compliance, Corporate Audit, Commercial organisation including clusters and categories, specialist areas (such as IT, Treasury, Tax, Enterprise support etc)		
1,2		Locations	— Location of operations globally (offices, sales offices and factories/distribution centers including addresses and number of personnel		
1,3		JV's	— Overview of Joint Ventures & Associates		
1,4		Auditor rotation	— Detail of Auditor Rotation requirements impacting the Group		
1,6	**XYZ Group structure**				
1,61		Organisation	— Organization chart, showing key individuals, responsibilities and reporting lines including Finance, Compliance, Commercial organisation including clusters and categories, specialist areas (such as IT, Enterprise support etc).		
1,62		Locations	— Location of operations globally (offices, sales offices and factories/distribution centers including addresses and number of personnel		
2	**Key Financial data**				
2,1		LE vs Reporting Unit	— Group structure chart and how it compares to the structure in the financial reporting system.		
2,2		Statutory Accounts	— Latest statutory accounts of entities requiring an audit for last 2 years **(available via a link to the existing database)**		
2,3		Statutory Accounts	— Break down by Legal Entity all entities requiring an audit (indication whether statutory, regulatory and group reporting fees)		
2,4		Audit Fees	— 2016/17 Audit Fees, Non-Audit and Consultancy fees by Reporting Unit		
2,5		Key figures	— Key Figures by Reporting Unit (NNS, GM, OP1, OP2, OP3 Net Assets etc)		
2,51		Key figures	— Consolidated view inclusive of central entries and inter co eliminations		
2,52		Key figures	— Local package amount		
3	**Financial results for the last 2 years**				
3,1		Key figures	— Break down of revenue and operating profit (before and after tax) by Reporting Unit		
3,2		Performance Matricies	— Explanation and calculation methodology of the MHC indicies		
3,3		Key figures	— Goodwill/intangible Assets by Reporting Unit		
3,4		Balance Sheet	— Balance Sheet by Reporting Unit		
3,41		Balance Sheet	— Consolidated view inclusive of central entries and inter co eliminations		
3,42		Balance Sheet	— Local package amount		
3,6	**MHC Group Financial results for the last 2 years**				
3,61		Key figures	— Break down of revenue and operating profit (before and after tax) by Reporting Unit		
3,62		Statutory Accounts	— 2016/17 Audit Fees, Non-Audit and Consultancy fees by Reporting Unit		
3,63		Balance Sheet	— Balance Sheet by Reporting Unit		
3,64		Key figures	— Key Figures by Reporting Unit (NNS, GM, OP1, OP2, OP3 Net Assets etc)		
4	**Group reporting and consolidation**				
4,1		Reporting timetable	— Indicative reporting dates and detailed year end timetable (2018)		
4,2		Reporting tool	— Example reporting package		
4,3		Reporting updates	— Quarterly Reporting Letters for 2017 & 2018		
4,4		Compliance	— Description of SOX process and example of SOX Certificate		
4,5		Consolidation process	— Description of the month end and year end consolidation process. Process notes to include how intercompany transactions and balances are processed		
4,6		Consolidation process	— Process for approval of top side journals		
4,7		Compliance	— Reporting package definitions		
5	**Standards and manuals**				
5,1		Standards	— Policy on Auditor Services		
5,2		Standards	— Financial Reporting and Control Policy		
5,3		Standards	— Accounting Policy Manual		
5,4		Standards	— Accounting policy updates as published during previous 2 years		
6	**GBS (Shared Service Strategy)**				
6,1		Shared Service	— GBS organization		
6,2		Shared Service	— Details of GBS sites, organisations and functionality		
6,3		Shared Service	— Scope of each site		
6,4		Shared Service	— Detail by market of Shared services provided by both internal and external providers		
6,5		Shared Service	— GBS quality and internal control processes		
7	**E2E Business Excellence**				
7,1		E2E Org	— Detail of organisation by E2E stream		
7,2		E2E projects	— Project charters for all active and planned projects by stream		
7,3		E2E strategy	— Transition planning strategy		
8	**Audit Committee/ Board papers**				
8,1		Audit Committee	— Executive management and Audit Committee meeting dates		
8,2		Audit Committee	— Audit Committee Agendas (and attendees) for last 2 years		
9	**MHC Internal Audit**				
9,1		Internal Audit	— Charter		
9,2		Internal Audit	— Plan		
9,3		Internal Audit	— Corporate audit reports for key group processes for last 1 year		
9,4		Internal Audit	— Group audit department structure, responsibilities and reporting lines		
9,5		Internal Audit	— Key audit risks		

Data Room

The first step in the process of creating your data room is, of course, your choice of data room provider. I sought the help and guidance of our M&A team in this regard, relying on their extensive experience of working with several providers.

There are many potential providers, all of whom will assure you of the security and user-friendliness of their proposed application.

In arriving at your choice of provider it is important to first decide what the key attributes of your chosen data room should be. There were six attributes that I was looking for; these were:

a.   Security (to be validated by our in-house IT security team)
b.   Option to restrict download to selected files
c.   Speed of accessing files
d.   Price (normally fixed up to a certain number of pages)
e.   Q&A functionality, ensuring all questions were blind to external users as to the questioner whilst providing full transparency and visibility to all users of the question and responses
f.   Reporting functionality available to the PM (enabling me to firstly monitor the data loads and then to monitor the activity in the data room of all users)

In my case four potential providers were asked to pitch for the assignment, all having been provided with the above list of key attributes we were looking for.

All four potential providers proposed solutions of an exceptional quality; indeed, of the six criteria I had set all were close on five, whilst the chosen solution delivered on all six, specifically excelling in the area of Q&A.

The security inherent in the solution was highly regarded by our internal security team and at the end of our process we were provided with an archive of all information.

The provider's team were always available (24/7) to address questions of the internal team as they populated the data room and provided a 30-minute training session on its use to each of the participating firms prior to going live.

The weekly reporting to me as project manager both during the build and post go live of the data room ensured I was able to maintain a strong visibility of use of the data room and subsequent questions during the process.

Having chosen the provider and created an index of information to be loaded, it is important for the PM to identify and secure the support and engagement of the contributors of the required information to be loaded into the data room. In achieving this you will absolutely need the support of your Group CFO in ensuring the identified resources. Treat this with the appropriate level of priority that their own line managers acknowledge and support.

For most of the contributors, the data room and its functionalities will be a new experience. To address this the provider's training needs to focus on how to load files and on the use of the Q&A function.

The PM should closely manage the data load period, setting the timelines to be followed and closely monitoring progress against these.

The quality and completeness of data loaded into the data room is key to the delivery of a transparent and comprehensive process. In order to ensure this the PM should review all the data, actively challenging the quality if he feels it is unclear or likely to cause confusion. Classic causes of confusion are often the prevalence of acronyms, which whilst commonly used by the company or the function using them, are likely to be incomprehensible to the firms' personnel.

In order to add to a robust review of the data, I found an effective model was to gather all contributors in a room, ask everyone to ensure they are not sat next to anyone from their own department/function. Then advise them that they should shake hands with the person sat on their right because over the coming week they will be required to review and give feedback on the quality and clarity of the data that person has loaded.

These peer reviews proved invaluable. If our data is not clear to a person familiar with the company, but not the function, then how are the firms' personnel going to understand it?

During our load period, we loaded 55,000 pages of information into the data room. You should never underestimate the effort required to collect the information, but even more importantly to ensure it is delivering a data set which is clear, concise and intuitive for the end users.

Depending on the size and complexity of the company, the tendering firms will put in place a large team to support their tender, all of whom will require access to your data room. In my case each firm had an average of 75 people participating.

A simple template should be provided to the firms to request access. This should be circulated at the same time as the data room index.

Below is the template I used to collect the requests for access:

MHC Group Audit Tender
Access to data room form

Name of Firm [   ]

People requiring access:

	Name	email address	Job Title	Role
1				
2				
3				
4				
5				
6				
7				
8				
9				
10				
11				
12				
13				
14				
15				
16				
17				
18				

Authorised signatory of tendering firm [   ]

NB: Role is either Input or Moderator or both

Many data room solutions have an inbuilt functionality whereby you can limit the number of questions that can be raised by each firm, by day, week or the end-to-end process. I, perhaps courageously or possibly out of blind stupidity, chose not to place any limit on the number of questions.

However, my decision was largely influenced by another inbuilt control that I chose to rely on towards ensuring only relevant and quality questions were raised.

This control required all firms to appoint moderators who would review and approve all questions raised by that firms' personnel, prior to them going live in the data room.

It was also made clear to the firms' Lead Partners that the quality and relevance of their questions would be an indicator of the quality of their team. It was also made clear that there were no "stupid questions"; therefore, the converse of the indicator as to the quality of the firms' teams was the quality of the information we loaded into the data room. It is worthy of note that over the course of our tender, we received a grand total of nine questions!!, three of which related to files a firm was unable to open.

In order to ensure the quality of answers was given the same degree of review as was the case with the original questions, the PM was moderator of all answers. As a result, only when an answer was approved would it become live and viewable by all the firm's teams.

In advance of the data room going live it is highly beneficial to you and your data room provider to organize a short on-line training session with each of the firm's teams. Your data room provider should be happy to provide and facilitate this.

The go-live of the data room signifies the formal start of the tender process. Further data loads should be minimal and primarily in response to questions.

In order to maintain the momentum of the internal team the PM should provide weekly reports, showing activity of the firms as they navigate their way through the data.

IT/Data Analytics workshop

Fundamental to the firm's understanding of the company and its ability to plan and provide an informed tender will be its understanding of the company's IT environment and the platforms on which it resides.

It will also be important to share with all the firms the company's position with regard to security restrictions which may impact on your willingness to allow the firms to utilize their audit analytics solutions within your IT environment.

Where the company has developed its own data analytics solutions in support of its internal monitoring of the control environment, it is also worth demonstrating these to the firms.

A good solution to address the sharing of these topics is to host a workshop for each firm. To be of enough value these workshops should ideally be held prior to the formal commencement of your tender process during the latter part of the preparation phase.

By following this suggested timing, all firms will have a strong understanding of the systems and control in place in the company such that they will be able to prepare for a future opportunity to demonstrate the audit tools which they have developed in advance of being given access to the data room and prior to commencing visits to the operations of the company.

Attendees from the company should represent the IT function including those responsible for IT security, the internal control team and representatives of the finance function.

Depending on the complexity of the company's IT environment, it is worth allocating a full day to each of the firms for the workshop. This will ensure adequate opportunity for good discussion and a robust Q&A. The firms should also be allocated some time during the workshop to enable them to showcase some of their solutions around data analytics and audit management portals.

All firms will likely have their own bespoke solutions. These are often very similar, although the defining points are how long they have actively used the tools in live audit engagements, and possibly more importantly, how they apply them. This discussion can become something of a sales pitch. My advice would be: in the same way you would challenge a statement from a car salesman when told a car is the best in its class, challenge the firms to substantiate claims they make around their tools.

It is also important to assess how much effort will be required from the company's IT function in assisting in the installation of the tools on to your IT environment. It is also essential that the company's IT team need to assess how the proposed solutions would impact the performance of your IT environment.

From the perspective of both the company and the firms, it is highly advised that those people who routinely work with the tools and the audit process are included in the attendees to the workshop in order to add to the relevance of the discussions. In my case I found, in general, the best discussions occurred during an informal buffet lunch during the workshops, as during this time people felt less inhibited in asking questions and challenging each other.

The outcome of the workshop should be a clear understanding of the IT environment of the company and a clear appreciation of the suitability of the proposed solution as well as an understanding by the firms of the anticipated future IT developments and how the IT landscape is expected to evolve over the coming years.

The agenda for the workshops should be the same for all firms, as indeed should the attendees from the company.

Below is the standard agenda I used for the workshops I managed:

IT, Digital Audit and Centralized Data Analytics Workshop

MHC has over the past years rolled out SAP to most of its entities across the world, under the organization titled "One-SAP".

Given the importance of ensuring all firms have a solid understanding of the IT infrastructure in MHC, a half-day workshop will be held.

This workshop is intended to provide a forum for representatives of our One-SAP team to explain our infrastructure both now and as it will evolve in the coming years. It will also be an opportunity for MHC to explain how Centralized Data Analytics has evolved, as well as how it is leveraged, both internally and by our current audit provider.

MHC has developed its own range of Data Analytics scripts which will be available to the audit firm to support its extraction requirements.

As Data Analytics is seen as a key component of our audit, it is proposed that during this workshop each firm will be able to present its own approach to digital audits and innovation in this area.

The workshops are expected to last for approximately four hours and each firm is asked to provide the names of those members of the firm best suited to attending.

The agenda for these sessions will be as follows:

IT in MHC
- Overview and history of the One-SAP programme
- IT Strategy
- Major IT projects in progress or already planned for delivery in the next 5 years
- Systems landscape based on SAP technology
- Systems landscape not based on SAP technology
- Major local and regional systems
- IT Governance
- Current context of the Global IT teams of MHC

Overview and demonstration of financial control analytics in MHC
- Scope and strategy for financial control analytics
- External audit view (aka Data Analytics for external audit)
- Internal control view (aka Data Analytics for internal control)
- Analysis of manual journals
- Analysis of open line items

Tendering firms
Overview of firm's approach to Digital Audit, solutions and scope impacts

Demonstration of how the firm uses Digital Audit in other assignments

How will your firm bring additional insights/value to MHC through your approach to a Digital Audit?

The agenda for the workshop should make clear the expected deliverables of all participants and should be included with the Audit Briefing provided in advance of the workshop.

All company participants should also be asked to sign an NDA, the firm's representatives being bound by the NDA in place for its employees.

To: MHC S.A.

Internal Confidentiality Statement – PROJECT TENDER

1.   As a member of the MHC project team for the Group Audit Tender (Project Tender), I understand that it is of great importance to MHC S.A. (which together with its subsidiaries and affiliates is herein referred to as the "**MHC Group**") that the secrecy of Project Tender and the confidential nature of information relating to the proposed process is maintained and protected at all times.

2.   In order to protect and maintain the secret and confidential nature of the information referred to in paragraph 1 above, I undertake as follows:

(i)   not to disclose to anyone other than a member of the project team as notified to me by Mr T Bryan, Head of the Group Accounting and Reporting any information which I see or which comes into my possession concerning Project Tender or the MHC Group's strategy regarding its selection of an external audit firm;

(ii)   not to disclose or discuss the existence of, or any details concerning, Project Tender to anyone other than a member of the Project Team;

(iii)   to refer any inquiries which I may receive concerning Project Tender (whether from within MHC or from external sources) to Mr T

Bryan without making any comment to the person(s) from whom the inquiry is received; and

(iv) to comply with the terms of the confidentiality agreement to be entered between MHC S.A. and the tendering firms a copy of which is attached to this Confidentiality Statement.

3. If I become aware that I or any member of the MHC Group may have to disclose information concerning Project Tender in order to comply with any legal or similar requirements, I will immediately bring this issue to the attention of Mr T Bryan.

4. The obligations contained in paragraph 2 above shall cease to apply to any information or knowledge which:

(i) may subsequently come into the public domain, other than by way of unauthorized disclosure;

(ii) I can show was previously known to me free of any obligation to the MHC Group;

(iii) is disclosed by the MHC Group to third parties without restriction; or

(iv) is received by me from a third party where such disclosure does not breach an obligation of confidentiality to the MHC Group.

If I am in any doubt as to my obligations under this statement, I shall consult with Mr Graham Hall as to the appropriate course of action.

This undertaking shall be governed by the laws of xxxx without regard to its principles of conflict of laws.

Signed:
Date: , 20XX
Name:
Title:

MHC Group Audit Tender Process
Note to all participants to the process

Governance principles

The MHC Group Audit Committee has requested FRA to commence a tender process covering the MHC Group Audit; all MHC participants will be required to sign the attached Confidentiality Statement.

The Audit Tender process is a highly confidential and emotive subject. For this to be successful, it will require that we adopt a transparent, open approach to all tendering firms, being respectful of the significant investment in terms of time and effort they will put behind their tender.

MHC will share significant previously undisclosed information to a wide community of external participants from the tendering firms; to this end all tendering firms will also be required to sign individual Non-Disclosure Agreements (NDA).

With regards to the MHC internal community, those acting on the project team and those identified as "key contributors" as well as all members of the management community who will have cause to interact with the tendering firms will need to follow strict protocols.

These protocols are intended to ensure all participating firms have access to the same level of information and are also seen to be ensuring access to key decision makers is balanced and fair on all tendering firms.

All members of the project team and the key contributors will be required to respect the protocol of confidentiality; this would inherently mean that no information, documentation or anecdotal information of which they have become aware during the project may be shared outside the project team.

Similarly, during any interaction that project team members may have with participating firms during the process, it is essential they remain mindful of the need for a balanced tender process and as such not to share any information not widely available to the other tendering firms which could place a firm in a position of advantage.

All market visits, dialogue with the management community as well as members of the Audit Committee will be coordinated by the project manager (PM), thus ensuring all firms are acting on a balanced "playing field".

Where a tendering firm asks for specific non-planned access to management or to information not foreseen to be disclosed in the tender process, this will be coordinated by the PM with similar access being afforded to the other firms, should they wish to avail themselves of the opportunity.

In addition to this internal protocol, all tendering firms will be expected to respect the process and communication channels.

To this end, except as communicated and planned by the PM, members of the tendering firms (both regarding the central tender team and that firm's local representation) should have no unplanned direct interaction with MHC personnel; this will ensure no competitive advantage is perceived from these interactions.

A market visit agenda will be provided to all tendering firms. This will outline the dates available for each market to be visited; it will then be for the tendering firms to elect which markets they wish to visit. The PM will coordinate and attend all visits and ensure these are conducted in a timely fashion with each firm being afforded a full day or part thereof each for their visit.

Obviously, the intent is to ensure each tendering firm is kept separate during market visits whilst at the same time not placing too high disruption on local MHC management.

In order to provide a meaningful forum for the firms to adequately showcase their various tools it may be helpful to both sides to schedule a second workshop towards the end of your process. This will enable the firms to adapt their tools to the company's environment and in doing so address any security concerns or learnings following the first-round workshop.

Consideration should also be given to providing the firms with an extract of the company's data. This will enable them to provide a meaningful demonstration of the output of their tools and proof that their use is a reality.

Both workshops should ideally be attended by the same representatives to ensure continuity. The firms will, of course, ensure their best IT and analytics experts are present to ensure a "meeting of minds" between the IT experts from each side.

After each workshop, those attending on behalf of the company should complete an assessment questionnaire.

IT Workshops Evaluation Matrix

Proposal Criteria	Points	Firm A	Firm B	Firm C	Firm D
The audit firms approach is tailored towards obtaining an understanding of MHC's activities, operating systems, personnel and specific needs, whilst also being tailored to both the size and complexity of MHC.	0-5				
The proposal demonstrates both a strong understanding of data analytics as a key component of an effective audit, whilst also showing a desire to place significant reliance on centrallised data analytics as a driver towards efficiency of the audit process.	0-5				
The team demonstrates a colaborative yet independent mindset, along with a sound understanding of MHC, its goals and aspirations.	0-5				
The proposed firm demonstrates the strengths of its team members as well as their years of prior experience in the particular industry and type of engagement that MHC represents.	0-5				
The audit firm understood the parameters within which data analytics can be applied to MHC systems and were able to address all points highlighted in the Audit Tender Solution Assessment.	0-5				
The firm clearly explained how the audit approach will enhance the overall MHC control Environment	0-5				
Does the solution used by the audit firm bring data analytics for External Audit / Internal control to the next level in terms of effectiveness, both from a content point of view (scope of scripts) as well as technology (predictive analytics, outlier's selection, exceptions management)	0-5				
The firm demonstrates both a strong understanding of data analytics as a key component of an effective audit, whilst also showing a desire to place significant reliance on centrallised data analytics as a driver towards efficiency of the local audit process.	0-5				
The firm clearly demonstrate an understanding of the MHC IT evolution add asked relevant and pertinent questions	0-5				
The firm demonstrates a clear understanding of the local MHC Risk profile and would tailor its audit approach accordingly	0-5				
The firm understands the MHC Audit requirements and has both the resources and experience to meet these	0-5				
The Partner clearly demonstrates a strong desire to drive efficiencies in the audit process coupled with an understanding of cost effectiveness of the process. The firm outlined there bespoke approach to Audit Analytics and how this will complement/enhance MHC Data Analytics	0-5				
The team demonstrates an empathy with MHC management such that a sound collaborative working relationship would be built over time enabling mutual respect within the boundaries of an auditor/client relationship	0-5				
Total Points	0	0	0	0	0

The output should then be consolidated and presented in graphical format for inclusion in the final briefing to be provided to the selection panel in advance of the first-round oral presentations at the end of the process.

It may be interesting to understand the evolution of each firm's scores between each of the workshops and to add a brief commentary to these when sharing with the selection panel.

Market Briefing

As outlined earlier, the operational aspects of the company, its people, brand portfolio, routes to market, footprint and risk and control environment are fundamental to defining the audit requirements of the company.

To this end all firms should be afforded equal opportunities to visit a selection of markets and meet the local teams. In order to facilitate this and ensure the full unrestricted engagement of the finance community in those markets, a briefing on the tender process should be provided to all impacted CFOs and subsequently shared with their finance leadership.

This briefing does not need to be as comprehensive as the one provided to the audit firms but should include a clear summary of the planned process, why the company has chosen to undertake a tender and an outline of the agendas and deliverables for each visit.

The market briefing should ideally include the following sections:

- Management Summary
  - o   Success factors
  - o   "what matters to you and your colleagues"
- Governance
- Timelines
- Post-visit evaluation
- Visit agenda
- Visit plan and associated logistics

The management summary is a key element, as it should clearly set out all phases of the tender and in many respects, it is your opportunity to ensure management in the markets feel part of the decision process and thus fully engage in its delivery.

At the end of the day you are asking the tendering firms to devote considerable resources and investment in the process, so the company should respect this and ensure its people are similarly committed. In delivering this commitment, the briefing should ensure the local finance community see themselves as a key contributor to the final decision and not merely reacting to the demands of the Group's Audit Committee.

This, of course, requires all markets to devote a lot of time and resources to the visits; this should be recognized in the briefing. However, to add weight to the message the briefing should also be copied to the Group CFO as a means of enforcing the message.

The sharing of the timelines should start the process of locking the dates and times of the market visits; thus, early circulation is important in order to avoid agenda conflicts.

I will cover the market visits in more detail later and my only comment at this point is that they are key to the process, demanding on all participants but also fulfilling and motivational at the same time. The sharing of the timelines also makes clear to all the level of commitment of the organization to the process, not only demonstrating the level of preparation but also the need for active participation of senior management.

The document below was the management summary I prefaced the Market Briefing document with. It tries to provide local management with a clear vision of the process and what is expected from them:

Management Summary

The MHC Group Audit Committee has requested FRA to prepare for a tender process covering the Audit of all MHC Group entities.

Following confirmation of the requirement to tender by the CCGC, the project team will be in place for October 2018 to enable adequate time for meaningful preparation and planning for the official commencement of the tender process in February 2019.

The formal tender process will then run for four months inclusive of opportunities for tendering firms to visit key material markets and subsequently to present to MHC their proposal.

The MHC Audit has not been subject to competitive tendering for a considerable number of years. The size of MHC, the geographical spread, the wide product range as well as regulatory requirements such as mandatory audit firm rotation in different jurisdiction and restrictions on non-audit services are reasons why a change of audit firm is a complex task. It clearly needs to be ensured that a change of audit firm is executed in a way minimising the risk to MHC.

MHC and the incumbent firm have worked together over the last several years to centralize the audit approach by systematically leveraging the Group GLOBE IT infrastructure, using Centralized Data Analytics.
As a result, the audit has delivered opportunities for a sustained reduction of the base fee.

The total fees agreed for the 2018 audit of the Group scope entities is in the region of USD XXm with a relatively flat fee of USD Xm for the remaining entities not in scope for Group Audit but requiring a Statutory or Fiscal Audit. Further downward pricing is expected.

Scope of a tender

A tender will encompass three elements:

1) The Group Audit scope, covering the sign off of the Group's published Financial Statements for the full year (December) including the Statutory reporting of those entities.

2) Review opinion of the Half-Year Financial Statements

3) The Statutory Audits of all markets not forming part of the Group audit scope.

The tendering firms will thus be invited to define which reporting units they would require to include in the scope of works for the Audit Opinion of the MHC Group Financial Statements.

The tendering firms will also be open to define the Group and Component materiality within which their opinion will be framed.

Additionally, the Statutory Audits of all entities forming part of the Group will be included in the Tender.

The fee is expected to be comprehensive in nature and include provision for reasonable scope changes.

The tender submission is expected to provide for an itemized fee both by Reporting Unit for the Group scope audit and by Entity for the Statutory scope audits.

With regard to the Central fee element, this should also be split between the half-year review and the Annual Audit.

High-level Tender Process:

The process to select a new firm of external auditors will run for approximately 18 months including an effective tender process of circa 19 weeks, plus handover and on-boarding of the new appointee.

Any decision to rotate to an alternate firm will have implications associated with independence posed by our current use of all big 4 firms for non-audit services.

Following the decision to put the Group Audit out for tender, we need to start to prepare the competitive bid process during Q4 2018, such that we can present possible alternatives for approval to the Group Audit Committee in July 2019 (See high-level and detailed plan on following slides).

‾ A new firm would formally take over the Audit for the financial year ending 31st December 2020, from the date of the AGM in April 2020. During the second half of 2019 there will be a need for close collaboration between the incumbent firm and the potential new audit firm to ensure a smooth handover.

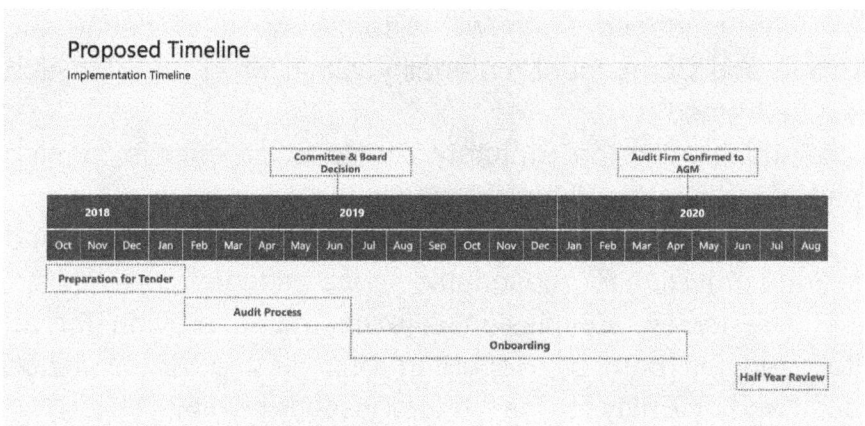

Proposed Timeline
Implementation Timeline

It is important to be aware of the inherent need of the appointed audit firm to ensure independence issues do not arise as a result of their appointment.

With regard to MHC expectation of future base Audit fees, there is a strong expectation that the agreed fee will reduce over time, from that agreed during the tender process due to efficiency gains. To this end we would expect the tendering firm to provide clear guidance as to areas where they would expect to deliver the required efficiency improvements.

The Group and local Statutory Audit fee will be set in USD, agreed at Group level and cascaded down to all entities.

Next steps

Following recommendation to tender by the Group Audit Committee, and approval thereof by the Board, including confirmation of the date by which the process should be completed, a project manager will commence the preparation phase of the project.

The outcome of the project is expected to provide a transparent, balanced recommendation to the Group Audit Committee enabling them to make an informed recommendation to the Board which will ultimately be ratified by the Shareholders at the next Annual General Meeting.

The briefing document is also the opportunity to share expectations for the feedback, post-visit, that each market will be asked to provide. This in itself enforces the message to the market finance community that they are key to the selection process.

During the tender process the role of local management is limited to the market visits, although this is, of course, central to providing the firms with ever more understanding of the business. The draft proposed agenda should be included in the briefing to aid the local teams with their preparation; the key message here would be that this standard agenda must be respected and replicated in full for all participating firms.

Market Visit Agenda

MHC

1. Overview of business
2. Products/categories
3. Locations/route to market
4. Legal structure
5. Management
6. SWOT
7. Performance
8. Balance Sheet
9. Intangible assets
10. Shared service usage
11. E2E
12. Audit expectations
13. Q&A

Tendering Firm

14. Overview of firm
15. Local organization
16. Resourcing & experience of your team
17. Introduction of local Lead Partner
18. Introduction of key members of the local team
19. Industry experience and client base in the country
20. How the firm leverages Data Analytics in its audit methodology
21. Areas you believe you can add value to MHC in this market
22. Your understanding of MHC risk profile
23. What is the firm's view of MHC?
24. Firm's view of F&B in the country
25. Explore any potential conflict of interest that should be considered (Partner or Senior Management engaged in Audit or Non-Audit work for an MHC competitor)
26. Q&A

Having provided the briefing to all relevant markets, follow-up calls with the local teams will help in clarifying expectation and maintain local buy-in to the process.

To address the Shared Service landscape, which in many organizations represents an ever-growing area of operations, it would be highly beneficial if visits to a selection of Shared Service Centers could also be incorporated into the visit plans.

A proposed agenda would be along the following lines:

MHC-BS Site Visit Agenda
MHC Business Services

1. Overview of MHC-BS organisation
2. Management
3. Scope of activities
4. Markets served and respective scope
5. SWOT
6. Planned expansion
7. Reporting (scope by market)
8. Q&A

Tendering Firm

1. Overview of firm
2. Local organization
3. Resourcing and experience of your team
4. Introduction of local Lead Partner
5. Introduction of key members of the local team
6. Industry experience and client base in the country
7. How the firm leverages Data Analytics in its audit methodology
8. Areas you believe you can add value to MHC in this market
9. Your understanding of MHC risk profile
10. Q&A

Key Functional Meetings

As part of providing the maximum exposure to the business for all firms to the central management of the company and its key functions, meetings should be scheduled where the function outlines its role and how the function brings greater focus to the risks associated to its area of responsibility. By setting up these meetings you will be able to address the need to bridge the knowledge gap of those firms not currently working closely with the company.

The scope of these meetings should be with senior finance functional leaders, for example, Group Accounting and Reporting, Treasury, Tax, Pensions and Internal Audit. It is also important to establish meetings with other functions likely to represent touch points of the audit, for example, Shared Services, Enterprise Risk Management or Procurement.

As with the market visits, the PM should attend all these functional meetings, including those held with the Group CFO.

As with the market visits, these meetings should be scheduled well in advance in order to avoid agenda conflicts and should be scheduled for a full day of meetings for each firm in order to reduce their logistics challenges.

These meetings are intended to provide opportunities for transparent sharing of information, but possibly more importantly, relationship testing. Are the firms able to communicate a clear message, does the firm bring technical experts able to understand and advise on the key risk areas associated with the function? Further, does the firm communicate a clear message which addresses potential audit issues in a manner which resonates with the function's management?

In my case we spread these meetings over a three-week period, being mindful that the function had other normal priorities to attend to. Each meeting was scheduled for ninety minutes.

Week one of these meetings was early in the process and was focused on functions with a likely material impact on the audit scoping plus an initial meeting for the proposed Lead Partner of each firm with the Group CFO.

The second and third weeks of meetings were planned to be held towards the end of the tender process and were directed at functions who actively participate in the audit process but not significantly impacting the scope or assessment of audit risk.

Intentionally, no specific agenda was planned for these meetings, the intent being to allow for open discussions to drive their own agenda. Inevitably, the questions and subsequent answers drove the flow of discussions such that they provided strong insight to the quality of each firm's understanding of the challenges and key audit risks surrounding the function.

It is enlightening to see the way each firm engages in such discussions and to observe the quality and relevance of the points they make and the way they ask their questions.

Given that each firm will bring their relevant subject experts to these meetings, it is equally important that the company ensure its own representation at the meetings comprises similar subject experts.

Again, a key measure of the meeting's outcome is an understanding of the quality of the firm's team and their personal fit to the culture of the company. Whilst the meetings are comparatively short, this due to the large number of functions to be included, the prompt attendance of all participants and with careful time management by the PM, the allotted time should enable the company attendees to formulate a clear opinion of the respective firms.

The exception to the single meeting opportunity afforded by the functional management meetings is the meeting with the Group CFO and the Head of Accounting and Reporting. In my case we combined the two and opted for an initial meeting at the commencement of the tender process, followed by a final meeting prior to the firms submitting their tender proposal.

The choice and selection of Audit provider is, of course, governed by the protocols of the Audit Committee who ultimately make a recommendation to the Board for ratification by shareholders at the Group AGM.

To this end it is highly desirable that all proposed Lead Partners of the respective firms are also afforded the opportunity to meet with the Chair of the Audit Committee. This will provide him/her with a forum to outline his/her expectations of the firm and to underline the governance principles within which the Audit Committee operates. It is noteworthy that the authority and influence of the Audit Committee, whilst being largely defined by regulatory guidance, can differ greatly from company to company.

As with the functional meetings, these meetings would have no set agenda, again allowing for the free flow of discussions. However, a one-to-one briefing was provided by the PM to each Lead Partner in advance of the meetings to ensure they were aware and prepared for the likely areas to be covered.

Naturally, whilst the Partner sought to impress, the CFO was focused on whether the potential relationship would be collaborative yet professional. In certain instances, the discussions were fairly in depth if on occasion hypothetical in nature. All Partners tried to ensure they were well prepared and perhaps it was the second session that afforded them the better opportunity to impress as they shared their own key learnings following four months of meetings with front line operational leaders and markets.

One would think the incumbent firm's proposed partner would be advantaged in these discussions owing to the inherent knowledge and understanding of the company provided by the firm's many years of being its auditor. However, the vision and opportunities offered by a fresh approach to the audit and an innovative mindset communicated by a partner who is new to the company can be incredibly compelling.

Following all meetings, the company representatives were asked to complete an assessment questionnaire, the output of which would be included in the overall assessment provided to the selection panel. It is important that this assessment questionnaire should be provided to the company attendees in advance of the meetings in order to act as a guide of the specific areas to be covered during the discussions.

The days assigned to each firm for these meetings are also an ideal opportunity for the PM to seek feedback from the firms on the tender process, what's working, areas needing more focus or access, whether they are comfortable with the level of engagement from the company. Such feedback should not be taken lightly. It will be many years until the company again tenders its audit; impressions can be lasting, so you and the company need to get it right.

The CFO and Head of Accounting and Reporting will also use their meeting to seek feedback on the process, more so given that they are relatively distant from the daily interactions with the firms during the tender process and are ultimately answerable to the Group Audit Committee for its effective and fair delivery.

Center Functional meetings Evaluation Matrix

Proposal Criteria	Points	Firm A	Firm B	Firm C	Firm D
Approach to Audit Quality					
The audit firms approach is tailored towards obtaining an understanding of MHC's activities, operating systems, personnel and specific needs, whilst also being tailored to both the size and complexity of MHC.	0-5				
The lead partner and his team demonstrate a strong understanding of MHC, its compliance culture and is clear on how his/her firm will ensure its audit methodology is able to address this	0-5				
Team Knowledge and Experience					
The Proposed Global Lead Partner demonstrates a colaborative yet independent mindset, along with a sound understanding of MHC, its goals and aspirations. He/she shows strong leadership skills being able to articulate a position with strenght and clarity	0-15				
The proposed firm demonstrates the strengths of its team members as well as their years of prior experience in the particular industry and type of engagement that MHC represents.	0-5				
The audit firm clearly demonstrated their audit firms commitment to professional training and staff continuity in line with our requirement of a maximum of 1/3 of the team rotating each year.	0-5				
The firm clearly explained how the audit firm's background, client base, licensing information and years in business make it well placed to provide value to MHC as its preferred audit provider.	0-5				
The audit firm has demonstrated its personnel are familiar with MHC's business in terms of our size, locations and strategic business goals.	0-5				
Data Analytics					
The firm demonstrates both a strong understanding of data analytics as a key component of an effective audit, whilst also showing a desire to place significant reliance on centrallised data analytics as a driver towards efficiency of the local audit process.	0-15				
Value Added Services					
The firm provided a listing of additional value added services the firm provides beyond the audit engagement. (e.g. proactively monitor and communicate topics relevant to our financial and business operations all year long that may impact our future success)	0-5				
Others					
The firm demonstrates a clear understanding of the local MHC Risk profile and would tailor its audit approach accordingly	0-5				
The firm understands the MHC Audit requirements and has both the resources and experience to meet these	0-5				
The Partner clearly demonstrates a strong desire to drive efficiencies in the audit process coupled with an understanding of cost effectiveness of the process. The firm outlined the competencies of its Technical Desk and how this will be available to support MHC	0-5				
The partner demonstrates an empathy with MHC management such that a sound collaborative working relationship would be built over time enabling mutual respect within the boundaries of an auditor/client relationship	0-20				
Total Points	0	0	0	0	0

Market Visits

Market visits provide essential additional insights of the company beyond that provided through the data room. Potentially of even greater importance is the opportunity afforded by the visits to provide for strong dialogue and interaction between the company's local teams and the tendering firm's proposed local audit team.

Whilst audit is subject to strong standards and guidelines, the personal aspect should not be overlooked; companies need a strong audit, but also, they need to be able to relate with and openly discuss matters with the audit team. A confrontational relationship does nobody any good and would likely dissolve any transparent discussions.

As such, the company and audit firms need to build a professional, collaborative relationship within the boundaries of never straying from generally accepted client/auditor professional independence.

The planning of market visits is a key element of the tender process. In my case the visits were spread over a ten-week period and covered approximately 55% of the Group's net sales.

The PM should attend all visits, his/her role being to facilitate and ensure all participating firms are exposed to the same level of information and the same personnel. The PM will also be available to set expectations of the visits and provide clarity on any point on which the local team are unclear. Aside from this the PM should take a back seat, whilst encouraging the local team and the firm's representatives to interact and share an open and transparent dialogue.

Whilst the agenda for the visits was shared in the Market Briefing (Chapter 8) there are several learnings from my own experiences that I would like to share, at this point, both from the perspective of the company and for a PM to be mindful of.

Firstly, the visit agenda will inevitably be demanding on the PM. In my case not only was I travelling extensively for ten weeks, flying over 86,000 miles and spending approximately 90 hours in the air, plus around 50 hours post-check in waiting for flight, I also did not get to see my family until all the visits were completed.

The demands on the tendering firms will, of course, be even greater, as they will likely return to base between visits. My own estimation was that each firm incurred costs in the region of USD5mio in participating in the tender.

It is also important to ensure continuity in the market visits. To this end only those attending the visits of all participating firms should be allowed to contribute to the post-visit assessments, thus ensuring we collect a balanced feedback not weighted by someone who only joined a limited number of the firm's visits.

One noted issue I identified during the market visits was that for the firm's nominated Lead Partner, it is important that they "lead" their team, guiding the discussions and demonstrably leading the firm's representation. I sometimes found that those firms currently not engaged in the audit allowed the current engagement partner, the person historically managing the relationship and consequently better informed about the company to the lead in all discussions. This tended to undermine the lead partner and leaves the company representatives with the impression that the proposed Lead Partner is both weak and not engaged.

This is a delicate balancing act. The inclusion of the engagement partner is for certain a positive addition to the team; they bring considerable knowledge and experience of the company; the firms should leverage this knowledge during the preparation and briefings. The fact that the engagement partner met with the local teams prior to each visit to explain the company and its culture was manifestly clear once the meetings began, leaving the company local team comfortable with the firm's local representatives. However, it needs to be made clear that the engagement partner takes a supporting role during the client-facing discussions enabling the Lead Partner to really lead the wider team.

Whilst the markets chosen to participate in the visits will represent the material elements of the business, the visits are also key to providing the firms with a clear understanding of the end-to-end processes and where and by whom these are performed.

Where the company has moved non-judgmental processes above market into internal or external shared service sites, then some of the material sites should be included in the planned visits.

In the case of the tender for which I was responsible, we visited three of the company's key shared service sites. These visits proved invaluable to building the firms' understanding of both our organization and where the key touchpoints of the audit were to be based.

In addition to explaining the above market usage by the business and its likely evolution in the coming years, these visits allowed the hitherto unsung youthful yet talented people working in above market sites to demonstrate their enthusiasm for the company and how their own brand of innovation is contributing to the wider goals of the company. This message really resonated with all of the firms.

The market visits also provide the firms with an opportunity to understand the company's DNA and through this gain a powerful insight into the values and behaviors that matter to it.

The relationship with the firm's local teams is, of course, fundamental and the proposed agenda provides the firm with enough time to demonstrate their strengths. Open dialogue underpins the visit agendas and should facilitate probing Q&A from both sides. One should be mindful that once the visits are finished the firms will need to prepare a proposal which outlines how, where and what they would audit, both in terms of the Group Scope Audit and the local Statutory or Regulatory audit requirements.

After the visits of all firms, the company's representatives were asked to provide their feedback. This is their opportunity to participate in the selection process.

The assessment template should be constructed to address the success factors that are relevant to the local audit team whilst also providing the local team's perception of the proposed Lead Partner.

Visits are often as enlightening for the PM as they are for the firms, even when the PM has worked closely with the local markets over many years.

It is likely that one element of the stated success factors which will resonate strongly with the company's management will be the proposed fee being underpinned by the delivery of efficiencies to the audit approach.

The visits are essential to support the firms in defining their proposed audit scope and work plan. Accordingly, the firms will need to gather the maximum intelligence possible to support the preparation of their proposal. Indeed, the visits will be the trigger by which the firms really start to visualize their proposed approach to the company's audit. Through this they will build their own vision of the scope and fees they will propose in respect of the engagement.

During the visits the firms will see for themselves the company's people and processes so that they understand how the local economic environment is impacting both business performance and its likely impact on the audit risk.

All firms will wish to communicate their particular "USP". The visits provide them with this opportunity to learn and at the same time test their approach to the audit on your local teams.

The firms, during their presentation to the company's local team, will often outline possible innovation approaches to the audit in order to gauge the reaction. It is key that in all the hype the company's local team seek to remove the mysticism and understand what is actually available, tried and tested and what is mere hyperbole and thus untested, undeveloped possible solutions, which, given a fair wind could be developed over the coming years.

Whilst the decision to launch a tender process may not have been driven by a perceived desire for change in the underlying audit methodology, it is inevitably a possible outcome; this could deliver significant economies.

At the commencement of the process the historic knowledge, which the incumbent audit firm brought to the discussions, was a clear advantage; however, this advantage quickly disseminated to potentially a disadvantage as they appeared less engaged and naturally asked fewer questions so that the dialogue was muted at best.

Post Market visit Evaluation Matrix

Proposal Criteria	Points	Firm A	Firm B	Firm C	Firm D
Approach to Audit Quality					
The audit firms approach is tailored towards obtaining an understanding of MHC's activities, operating systems, personnel and specific needs, whilst also being tailored to both the size and complexity of MHC.	0-5				
The local audit firms organisation and locations of its offices and personnel are sufficient to ensure a smooth and efficient delivery of the defined audit scope.	0-5				
Team Knowledge and Experience					
The Proposed Global Lead Partner and the Local Partner demonstrate a colaborative yet independent mindset, along with a sound understanding of MHC, its goals and aspirations. He/she shows strong leadership skills being able to articulate a position with strenght and clarity	0-15				
The proposed local team demonstrates the strengths of its local team members as well as their years of prior experience in the particular industry and type of engagement that MHC represents.	0-5				
The local audit firm clearly demonstrated their audit firms commitment to professional training and staff continuity in line with our requirement of a maximum of 1/3 of the team rotating each year.	0-5				
The local firm clearly explained how the audit firm's background, client base, licensing information and years in business make it well placed to provide value to MHC as its preferred audit provider.	0-5				
The audit firm has demonstrated its personnel are familiar with MHCs business in terms of our size, locations and strategic business goals.	0-5				
Data Analytics					
The firm demonstrates both a strong understanding of data analytics as a key component of an effective audit, whilst also showing a desire to place significant reliance on centralised data analytics as a driver towards efficiency of the local audit process.	0-15				
Value Added Services					
The firm provided a listing of additional value added services the firm provides beyond the audit engagement. (e.g. proactively monitor and communicate topics relevant to our financial and business operations all year long that may impact our future success)	0-5				
Others					
The firm demonstrates a clear understanding of the local MHC Risk profile and would tailor its audit approach accordingly	0-5				
The firm understands the local MHC Audit requirements and has both the resources and experience to meet these	0-5				
There are no apparent conflicts of interest represented by an appointment of this firm and independence issues are not significant	0-5				
The local partner demonstrates an empathy with MHC management such that a sound collaborative working relationship would be built over time enabling mutual respect within the boundaries of an auditor/client relationship	0-20				
Total Points	0	0	0	0	0

The three key points of difference I saw, which were absolutely linked to our communicated "Key Success Factors" were in the areas of:

(1)   People; how the relationships between the company and the firms (both Central representatives and the firms' local teams) evolved during the days, including how the teams engaged and sought to better understand the workings of the company in an open, professional and collaborative style.

(2)   The audit firm's approach to audit automation; the tools currently available to them, including how long they have been in use, and the way these would be applied and how they will be leveraged to assist the company in enhancing its control environment.

(3)   Opportunities to really add value to the company as the client; this could potentially include application of some of the tools the firms have developed which could enhance our control environment and providing key insights, leveraging sectors the firms are engaged in, for example shared services, sustainability and health sciences.

In some respects, the market visits are synonymous with multiple "dress rehearsals" in preparation for the eventual presentation to the selection panel.

Being aware that the company's representatives will provide their feedback on each firm as part of the process, the firms will often use their presentation and accompanying Q&A as an opportunity to cast doubt on the competing firms' ability to deliver on promised innovation. My advice to the local teams was to take this with a "large pinch of salt". The firms often went into sale mode, failing to focus on explaining their approach to the audit and instead trying to counter in a blind fashion any claim from competing firms.

In certain cases where such comment was less veiled and on occasion positively blatant, these were very badly reflected in the feedback assessment provided by the attendees.

Specific feedback included comments that they felt these behaviors were a sign of a firm desperate to counter the strengths of the competing firms and as such was indicative of a firm with low values and behaviors.

There are three key objectives of the market visits; firstly, to provide clarity on the business, building on the insights the firms have amassed through reviewing the information in the data room. Secondly, the visits are the opportunity for the company's local teams to the firm's local team who they would work with if the firm were to win the tender; through these interactions the company attendees are able to assess the relative strengths of each team.

Thirdly and of equal importance, the company's local teams will enjoy the opportunity to meet with the tendering firm's leadership team who are heading the tender pursuit. This includes the proposed Lead Partner. Through this they can provide the local perspective on the firm and their leadership.

Project Manager and the role of the Steering Committee

A full-time dedicated project manager (PM) is essential to your audit tender project, dependent on the size and complexity of the engagement being subject of the tender.

The role of the PM and his/her knowledge of and profile within the company is fundamental to the delivery of an effective tender process. He/she will need to reach out across the organization to ensure everyone is supportive of the process and makes him/herself available to deliver the visit and meeting agendas.

The PM should be a senior member of the Central Finance Community, having in all respects, a strong and deep-rooted knowledge of the business, the local market organizations and the key finance stakeholders. This will ensure that the wider finance community respect the process, its governance and key deliverables. The demands on the business and specifically the finance teams around the world will be significant, but with a strong PM supported by senior finance leadership in the center, it should prove possible to galvanize the business to engage in the process, with passion and energy which will prove infectious across all participants.

A close understanding of the current audit process, its scope and the Statutory and Regulatory audit requirements is also fundamental.

The position and responsibilities of the PM should never be underestimated. The PM is the face of the company to all participating firms; he/she sets the tone for your process. The PM needs to be empowered to drive the process whilst also enforcing the governance principles that have been defined.

As PM I prepared all the briefing documentation provided, including internally to senior management, those provided to the market CFOs in advance of the visits and the detailed briefing in support of the RFP provided to the tendering firms at the start of the process.

In my role as PM, I also worked closely with all those in the company who would engage with the firm's representatives once the tender process commenced. Through these discussions I was able to ensure an appreciation of the key role they would play in the selection process. Their support was essential in meeting the company's stated objective of delivering a fair, transparent and balanced process for all firms.

The support and empowerment of the PM by the Group CFO and Head of Accounting and Reporting provide an essential role, not only by acting as a foil to support the project governance, but also as a sounding board, able to challenge the PM as he/she defines the process and puts it into action.

An admin support to the PM is also essential. Their support in coordinating the meeting plan, ensuring security passes are available for the firms, appropriate meeting rooms are available so that you do not need to trail the representatives of the firms around your building but rather have those from the company who they are meeting come to a single meeting room, really simplifies the logistics.

The logistics of the market visits are also a significant call on your admin support's time; from organizing flights to hotels plus ground transportation and coordinating everyone's calendars, the admin role is a thankless task and a crucial one. My own admin support was exceptional, a view also shared by all the firms.

As previously outlined, the tender process is underpinned by a significant visit agenda as well as meetings with key functions having an impact on the audit risk and management of the control environment. The PM needs to be fully embedded in this element of the process, attending all meetings and monitoring the discussions to ensure all firms receive the same degree of engagement.

With regard to the PM's role in providing oversight of the Governance principles, the PM should not shy away from raising with senior management actual or suspected violations of these principles that he/she becomes aware of. The PM should be ever mindful of the risk to the company's reputation posed by members of the management community participating in side-bar discussions with firms with whom they have a longstanding non-audit relationship. Such discussions run the risk of unfairly disadvantaging the other firms by providing insight into areas of the business not shared wider; this could be on areas of additional risk or commercial challenges the company faces.

As with all key projects, a steering committee should meet regularly throughout the process; at these meetings the PM should provide an update on the process and seek guidance on any issue that arises.

In order to ensure that the Steering Committee members are kept closely informed on the content and learnings from the market visits, the PM should provide a brief summary at the end of each visit highlighting the engagement and participation of all those attending. This update should also provide an initial view on the local team's reaction to the firm's team and the presentation and tool which they demonstrated.

The Steering Committee will also be the forum through which the selection process is defined along with confirmation of the proposed selection panel for final validation by the Audit Committee. The Group Audit Committee who has final governance over the appointment of the Group Auditor should be regularly updated on the tender process; generally, this would be given by the CFO or Head of Accounting.

Complementary to the role of the Steering Committee and the Audit Committee, it is important that the wider finance organization feel party to the decision process and are therefore given a fair opportunity to contribute, ensuring the ultimate choice of audit firm is fully representative of the operational requirements of the Group. Accordingly, a summary of all of the feedback assessments provided during the fieldwork of the tender should be provided to the selection panel and the AC.

Feedback Assessments by
Business Key Stakeholders

As highlighted previously, it is important that the choice of your audit firm is not based purely on the opinions of the selection panel who will have limited opportunities to challenge and assess the firm's proposed audit methodology or indeed their central and local teams.

Obviously, in addition to hearing the firm's presentation to the selection panel, they will also, hopefully, have reviewed the firm's written proposal. However, I would challenge whether this constitutes full understanding of the firm, its people and its proposed audit approach.

The obvious answer is no, or at best only partially.

Both the company and the participating firms will have invested considerable time, money and resources in the tender process. This investment needs to be respected and should drive everyone to ensure the outcome takes full account of the effort and engagement of everyone.

If the ultimate decision does not take full account of the feedback collected following the functional meetings and market visits, then management risk at best missing the operational implications of the choice of audit provider and likely leaving the wider finance community feeling disenfranchised and thus irrelevant to the process.

It was for this reason and to ensure the full engagement of the wider finance community to the selection process that I decided (after alignment with the Steering Committee) to seek feedback from all internal touch points.

Whilst the assessments were based on five key measures which derived from the success factors identified by members of Senior Finance and the Audit Committee, the questions within each section were specific and relevant to the company's participants at each meeting.

Within these five sections there were thirteen questions, with respondents being requested to score each based on one to five (five being the highest ranking). On consolidation some of these questions were subject to an additional weighting in line with that identified in the success factors which senior management had deemed of the greatest importance to the company. These weightings were consistently applied across all assessments and were specifically discussed and approved by the Steering Committee.

In addition to the three assessments outlined in earlier chapters (Data Analytics Workshops, Functional Meetings and Market Visits), further assessments were provided by those reviewing in detail the written tender proposals of each firm. This was a simplified assessment based solely on the five key measures derived from the success factors; this again sought scoring against each of one to five, but in this instance no weighting was applied.

The written proposals provided in advance of the first-round selection panel are the first opportunity for the firms to outline how they would propose to audit the company, the scope of markets to be included and, of course, their fee proposal. This would cover both the Group Financial audit and the statutory audits of all remaining entities. Accordingly, the requested assessments covering these two phases in the process are intended to address these new and significant data points.

In an earlier chapter, I refer to the delivery of an audit tender as being in many respects "a journey of discovery"; this notion manifests itself as the PM collects the feedback assessments as the process unfolds and adds the output from across the company to the consolidated results.

The principle of all firms being equal from the start is problematic, given that the incumbent firm both is familiar with the company and has a significant understanding of the processes and people; the journey for the other firms sees their knowledge expand from the day the process starts with access to the data room. This then accelerates through the functional meetings, market visit and Q&A.

As I reviewed the submitted assessments during the process and added them into my consolidation workbook, it was noteworthy that the incumbent firm started out with very positive scores. However, as the process unfolded this advantage rapidly disappeared and the other firms' scores were consistently improving to the detriment of the incumbent firm.

One prevalent theme was in the area of innovation and the openness of those firms new to the Group to look at the future audit from a true "blank page" perspective, whilst the incumbent firm appeared hindered by the boundaries of their current audit approach.

This openness to change, coupled with innovation, especially in a company itself going through a period of significant change, clearly resonated with those at the operational level of the company, a fact which became clear in the evolving feedback and supporting comments.

The initial advantage became increasingly dissipated as the discussions on each firm's approach to the audit and the tools they would deploy towards greater audit automation were shared.

Maybe another factor which played to the advantage of the new firms was the fact of them being just that – "new".

This contributed to them displaying a keen and ever-present desire to learn – learn about the business, the portfolio and our people; in so doing they demonstrated a passion and a highly collaborative mindset.

The delivery of the written proposal is the first time many readers will have been exposed to the significant increase in understanding.

Below is the assessment all readers of the proposal were asked to complete; the questions are intended to be focused on what they see and take away from the proposal.

Audit Tender Written Proposal Evaluation Matrix

Proposal Criteria	Points	Firm A	Firm B	Firm C	Firm D
Approach to Audit Quality					
The written proposal clearly demonstrates the firms understanding of the priorities as outlined in the Success Criteria communicated in the briefing and outlines an audit approach which would deliver strongly against these.	0-5				
The written tender proposal clearly outlines the global footprint of the firm and identifies that its spread of offices and personnel is adequate to ensure delivery of our audit requirements across all geographies	0-5				
Team Knowledge and Experience					
The CV of the proposed lead partners and those of the key markets demonstrate the strength of the proposed team as well as their fit to the MHC world. The industry experience of the team is sufficient as to enable a quick understanding of the MHC Risk profile	0-5				
The personnel to be allocated to the audit and the time they will dedicate demonstrates a strong wish to work towards a smooth no surprise audit outcome	0-5				
The proposal highlights the audit firms commitment to professional training and staff continuity in line with our requirement of a maximum of 1/3 of the team rotating each year.	0-5				
The proposal provides the audit firm's background, client base, licensing information and years in business.	0-5				
The written proposal clearly outlines how the audit assignments will be resourced and how the firm will maintain continuity of those resources over time.	0-5				
Data Analytics					
The proposed solution for leveraging data analytics is in line with MHC expectations and respects our stated position with regards to access controls around MHC systems and data. The firm demonstrates both a strong understanding of data analytics as a key component of an effective audit, whilst also showing a desire to place significant reliance on centralised data analytics as a driver towards efficiency of the local audit process.	0-5				
Value Added Services					
The proposal provides a listing of additional value added services the firm provides beyond the audit engagement. (e.g. proactively monitor and communicate topics relevant to our financial and business operations all year long that may impact our future success)	0-5				
Scope and Pricing of the Engagement					
The written submission clearly outlines the proposed scope of markets to be included in the MHC SA audit, this scope would meet the requirements of the Group in so far as providing management comfort as to the integrity of the Consolidated Financial statements	0-5				
The proposal includes a fee by Reporting Unit outside the scope of the Group scope for the provision of Statutory/Regulatory audits to be performed in line with the Group guideline of completion by30th June of the subsequent year	0-5				
The tender proposal outlines the competencies of its Swiss Technical Desk and how this will be available to support MHC	0-5				
The proposed fee for the Audit of markets inscope of MHC SA is competitive in Nature and the fee relative to each market is clearly outlined, additionally, The partner demonstrates an empathy with MHC management such that a sound collaborative working relationship would be built over time enabling mutual respect within the boundaries of an auditor/client relationship	0-5				
Total Points		0	0	0	0

Having collected in the various assessments as the process evolved, it became interesting to prepare the consolidated feedback to the selection panel.

The creation of the charts showing both the feedback by assessment and a consolidated view was, of course, simple. The challenge was to provide impartial guidance on what was driving the scores.

As is often the case with regard to preparing a presentation that will likely be shared with key stakeholders without the opportunity for the preparer to speak direct to the topic, it is important to transmit a clear message, such that the reader can quickly draw their own conclusions as to the key takeaways. With too much information and detailed commentary, the message will be lost; with too little information and the reader is left wondering what message you are trying to convey.

The following slides are the approach I adopted in the selection panel briefing in advance of the first-round oral presentations by the firms. Obviously, I have removed both the names of each firm and the comments I added to the charts. I share these now to enable you to understand the level of information feedback shared.

In addition to the various graphs which show clearly both the most favored firm and the strength of each firm when measured against the stated success factors, I added a selection of the comments I had received from the contributors. In this regard I tried to take a balanced approach in selecting the comments I opted to include.

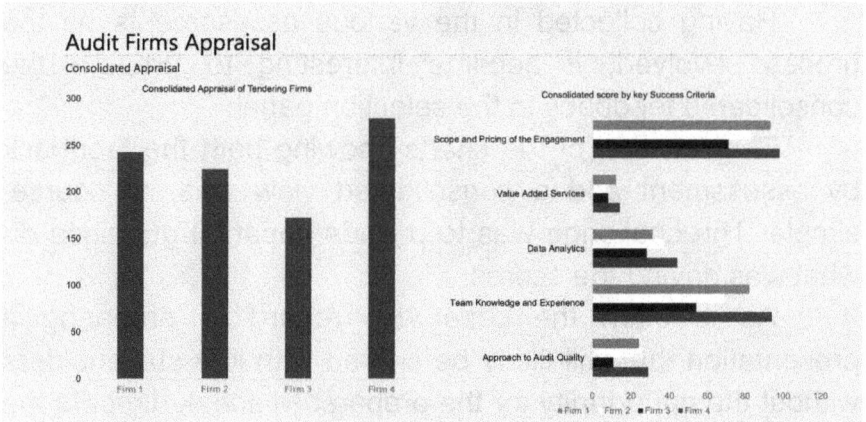

Audit Firms Appraisal
Consolidated Appraisal

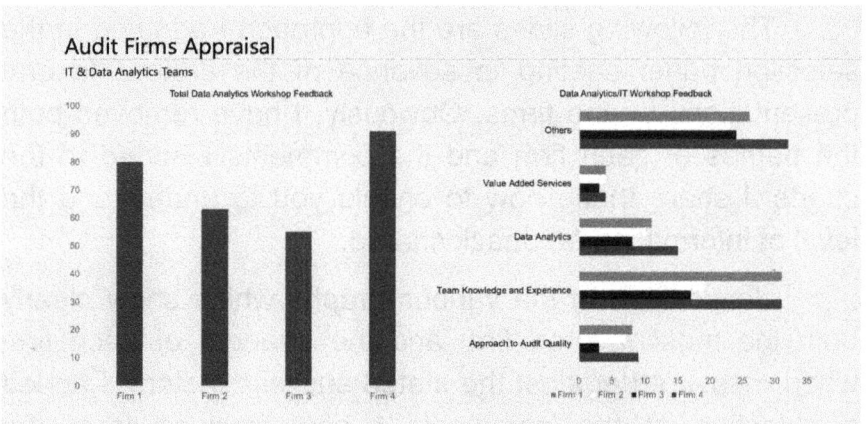

Audit Firms Appraisal
IT & Data Analytics Teams

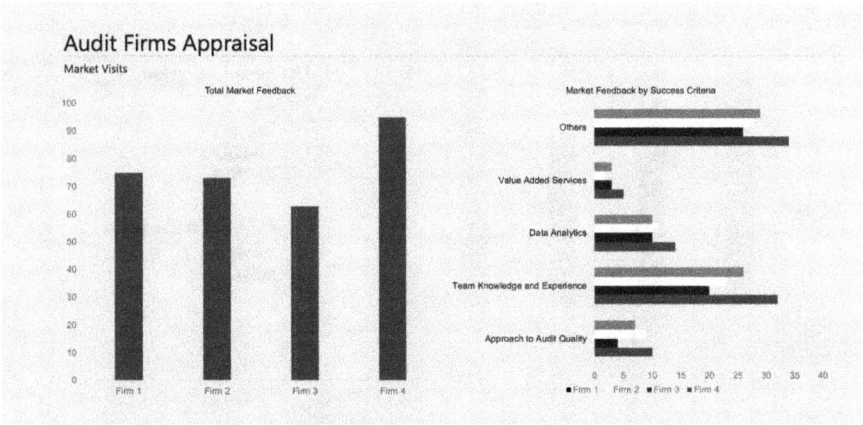

Audit Firms Appraisal
Market Visits

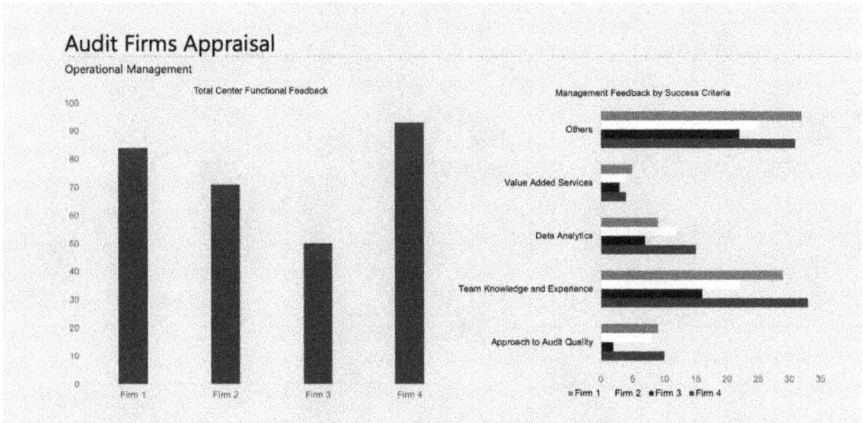

Audit Firms Appraisal
Operational Management

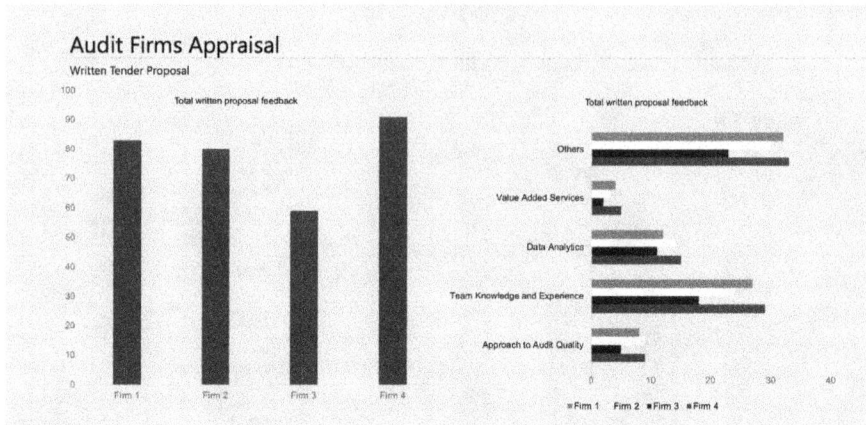

Audit Firms Appraisal
Written Tender Proposal

Written Tender Proposal

The quality of the written tender proposal is often indicative of how well the firms understood your business and indeed the briefing you provided at the outset. You should also be prepared to receive a classic, yet professional sales document.

The length of the proposal and the depth with which the firm outline their vision of how an audit of your company would evolve, were they to be selected, can be an absolute eye opener. However, the reader should take a deep breath, settle down in a quiet corner and review it with an open mind and a challenging mindset.

Typically, the written proposal will start by introducing the leadership team, their experience and credentials; this will then be followed by similar information on other key members of the central team and the proposed Partner and Senior Manager in the key markets.

The proposed Lead Partner will also, in most cases, introduce the proposal, in which they will passionately explain both what they will bring to the audit and how this approach will revolutionize and add value to the company. They will further explain how a digital automated audit will deliver significant benefits whist also talking about the quality of the firm's leadership and the wider teams. Some firms preface this introduction with a note from the firm's Global Head and or its Global Head of Audit Assurance. This is the firm's opportunity to demonstrate their commitment to your company and their support for the proposed Audit Leadership Team.

Some firms will as an alternative provide a video message by the Global Leadership.

Having experienced both approaches, I believe it is due to the Governance in place during the tender which prevented the firm's Global Leadership reaching out to the company's management which left them still wishing to communicate and be involved in their firm's pursuit.

So, turning once more to the content of the written proposal, what can you expect?

A sales pitch and multiple promises, but also some clear and compelling innovative solutions, the challenge is to separate the wood from the trees and identify the true strengths and weaknesses of each proposal.

The reader needs to critically assess the proposal and through this identify those points that need to be clarified, either prior to or during the first-round oral presentations.

Having read the introduction it is in the heart of the proposal that it gets interesting and the point at which each of the firm's proposals can be compared and calibrated. The firm will endeavor to explain how an audit performed by them differentiates them from all other firms. In the case of the tender I ran, the company was transitioning significant back office functionality above market into shared service centers. This was seen by some firms (but not all) as an opportunity to reimagine the audit landscape and through this refocus audit activities away from the markets to these centers where most transactions were booked.

Automation was also a key enabler of this new approach and the firms will seek to showcase the tools they would bring to your audit through the written proposal. Obviously, this is not an easy task. Fortunately, having held the IT data analytics workshops and received feedback from the company IT and data analytics experts after the workshop, it was possible to compare the written IT proposal alongside the feedback we collected and through this understand the acceptability of the technical aspects of the proposed solution.

In an ideal world this overview of a digitally enabled audit will be written in layman's terms, such that the reader can easily understand the proposed solutions and what this could deliver to the audit process.

A further defining element of the proposal is the scoping and component materiality levels to be applied to the audit activities relevant to the Group audit, whilst also being mindful of the requirements of local Statutory Audits of the remaining Group entities. Each firm will define those markets it would include based on several factors, for example, Net Sales, Operating Profit, Net Assets and Intangible Assets plus the level of risk relative to the business.

A further differentiator, which surprised me given the accepted methodology followed in its calculation, was each firm's proposed Component Materiality that it would apply. In the case of the audit proposals there was a spread between each proposal of 30%.

The above points also, of course, lead to the proposed fee; this does not necessarily need to be quoted by legal entity, although where it is tends to demonstrate the depth and robustness of the total fee proposal. In calculating the fee proposal, the firms will obviously be guided by current audit fees disclosed by entity in the data room. They will then factor into this any changes in scope or those changes in audit approach due to its plans to refocus the audit effort.

One additional consideration when assessing each firm and the respective merits of each of their proposals is the implications on independence were they to be appointed. All the big four firms, and indeed many others, offer significant non-audit and consultancy services. The Audit Committee of your company will have defined clear guidelines for both the approval of such services, but also specific guidance on the provision of such services by the appointed auditor of the company. Each firm's tender proposal should be clear in disclosing any non-audit or consulting services they provide and what independence validation process the firm have in place.

The proposal should identify any service that they believe would compromise these guidelines and their proposal to exit those services should they be successful in winning the appointment.

The potential independence issues, whilst a consideration should, however, not be allowed to preclude the appointment of that firm were they to be successful in the pursuit.

The written proposal of those firms not currently the auditor of the company will also include a section covering a high-level transition plan. This is an important section and represents an opportunity for you to understand the potential impacts on your organization of a change of auditors. It also provides further insight into each firm's understanding of the complexity of your company and the key touch points of your future audit given each firm's proposed audit approach.

The level of detail provided will likely differ considerably; the more convincing ones will provide a detailed list of actions along with timelines for their delivery. This section should be expected to also include a list of recent appointments each firm has won; this information, whilst not implicit in its disclosure, provides your management with a potential sounding board to whom they can reach out in order to validate the claims and credentials of each firm.

As mentioned earlier, digitalization of your audit may well be a priority for your company and as such an area of differentiation between each of the firms. The written proposal in the section covering the transition plan should include details about the deployment of the tools and methodologies each firm proposes to bring to your audit. This should provide further insight as to the degree of effort that would be required by your IT function to make implementation a reality.

The question of transition and the possible disruption this may represent to your company needs to be measured against the potential benefit a change could deliver. Indeed, there may well be a measurable change dividend which facilitates finance, a function often seen as change averse, driving standardization and automation across all levels of the company.

Obviously, all companies are different. The scope and location of activities, their footprint across the globe and legal entity structures in each jurisdiction will be factors which need to be considered by the firm in formulating its audit and transition plans.

To this end, the proposal may include an overview of the process to be followed in each legal entity where a change in auditor is to be made while one is conscious that legal and regulatory filings to implement the change of auditor can complicate matters. For example, some of your entities may be listed on the local stock market or may be a financing entity; in both instances they would be deemed "Public Interest Entities" (PIEs) and thus subject to regulations impacting audit firm rotation.

See below Global Transition requirements:

Europe

France

Specific regulations and requirements

1. In France, statutory auditors are appointed by the shareholders meeting for a six-year term.

    The client cannot dismiss the statutory auditor. Resignation can occur in limited situations.

    The same rules apply to the substitute statutory auditor, which is appointed at the same time as the statutory auditor.

Resignation of incumbent auditor

2. The statutory auditor cannot resign except for specific legitimate reasons provided by the French Code of Ethics. The following shall constitute a legitimate reason to resign:
    (a) The definitive discontinuance of business
    (b) Pressing personal reasons, on the grounds of health
    (c) Difficulties encountered in carrying out the engagement, which are impossible to resolve
    (d) The occurrence of an event that may compromise compliance with the professional standards applicable in France and impair the independence or objectivity of the statutory auditor.

On a practical level, in case of a change of auditor in the parent company:

•• The independence or objectivity of the statutory auditor might be impaired where the statutory auditor's network provides non-audit services to the parent company conflicting them as statutory auditor of the subsidiary

•• It might not be possible for the statutory auditor to carry out the audit engagement and perform all necessary audit procedures in satisfactory/ reasonable conditions if it appears, notably, that (i) incoming firm functions or processes are centralized and/or incoming firm controls are operated centrally, (ii) incoming firm cannot get access to such functions and processes nor get comfort on these controls through alternative procedures.

•• Beginning June 1, 2017, the statutory auditor that resigns must inform the Haut Conseil du Commissariat aux Comptes (French statutory auditors' oversight board) and indicate the reasons for its decision.

Appointment of INCOMING FIRM

3.   INCOMING FIRM and INCUMBENT FIRM to obtain authorization from company to communicate.

4.   INCOMING FIRM to send an acceptance letter prior to the shareholders' general meeting.

5.   The Audit and Risk Committee to advise the Board of Directors on the nomination of INCOMING FIRM.

    The shareholders to appoint INCOMING FIRM by the proposal of the Board of Directors.

6.   INCOMING FIRM to notify the Compagnie Régionale des Commissaires aux Comptes about nomination within eight days after the shareholders' meeting decision.

7.   Company to send to the court of registry the minutes of the shareholders' meeting and the declaration and acknowledgment of INCOMING FIRM. Company to publish the nomination.

8.   INCOMING FIRM to send a letter to INCUMBENT FIRM, asking them to confirm that their replacement is not due to points mentioned in article 21 of our Code of Ethics. INCOMING FIRM to obtain access to the working papers of INCUMBENT FIRM.

Germany
<u>Rotation</u>
1.   INCOMING FIRM audit partners must rotate after ten years for non-PIE (entities).
<u>Resignation of incumbent auditor</u>
2.   Company and INCUMBENT FIRM are required to inform and explain the reason to the chamber of certified public accountants (Wirtschaftsprüferkammer) on the termination and revocation of a current audit engagement.
<u>Appointment of INCOMING FIRM</u>
3.   Company to elect INCOMING FIRM as auditor at the annual general meeting.
4.   Supervisory Board (if any) to assign INCOMING FIRM as auditor.
5.   INCOMING FIRM to accept the engagement.

Italy
<u>Specific regulations and requirements</u>
1.   Statutory engagement letters cover a three-year period.
<u>Rotation</u>
2.   For non-PIE there are no rotation rules for the audit firm; instead the engagement leader must rotate off after 10 years (with some exceptions).
<u>Resignation of incumbent auditor</u>
3.   The audit committee initiates the assessment of potential alternative auditors. The audit committee must submit to the shareholders' meeting a reasoned/ motivated proposal for the appointment of INCOMING FIRM.

The audit committee assessment is mandatory, but management can decide whether to adhere to it or not.

4. In case of early termination, company must notify INCUMBENT FIRM of its decision to change auditor for just cause (to be disclosed); the change of the group auditor is a common just cause to change the local auditor.

5. INCUMBENT FIRM to notify company its observations in relation to the early termination of the audit contract.

    The early termination of a statutory audit engagement can be carried out by means of:
    •• Revocation of the engagement for a valid cause
    •• Resignation of the statutory auditor (for a valid cause)
    •• Termination by mutual consent of the audit contract (generally not suggested by INCOMING FIRM Italy).

6. INCOMING FIRM to submit the proposed audit contract to Company.

7. The shareholders' meeting to examine the proposal made by the BoD, the observations made by INCUMBENT FIRM and the audit committee, revoke INCUMBENT FIRM and appoint INCOMING FIRM considering the reasoned proposal made by the audit committee.

8. A copy of the resolution of the appointment of the INCOMING FIRM to be filed with the client register.

9. INCUMBENT FIRM to notify the Ministry of Economics of observations in relation to the revocation within 15 days from the date of the delivery.

10. Within 15 days from the date of the shareholders' meeting, Company to notify the Ministry of Economics of the early termination of the audit contract together with a copy of the relevant documentation (audit committee report and INCUMBENT FIRM's observations, BoD report, shareholders' meeting resolution).

Appointment of INCOMING FIRM

11. Company to notify INCOMING FIRM and provide a copy of the shareholders' meeting minutes with the appointment).

12. Company to sign INCOMING FIRM engagement letter.

13. Company to sign clearance letter to INCUMBENT FIRM.

14. INCOMING FIRM to receive signed clearance letter from INCUMBENT FIRM.

15. Once the letter is received, INCOMING FIRM to get in touch with INCUMBENT FIRM to plan a working paper review.

Luxembourg
Specific regulations and requirements

1. The audit services can only be provided by a Réviseur d'Entreprises Agréé (approved statutory auditor). The audit profession is regulated by EU Regulation 537/2014 and EU Directive 2014/56/EU.

Rotation

2. No firm rotation requirements for non-EU PIE.

   For EU PIE, after ten years of service, Company must set up a public audit tender and, in case of a win by INCUMBENT FIRM, the service tenure may be extended by another ten years. Maximum period of appointment – 20 years.

   There are specific transitional rotation requirements for the auditors of EU PIEs, which were already the auditors as of 16 June 2014.

Resignation of incumbent auditor

3. INCUMBENT FIRM may resign during the term of appointment. In such case, Company and INCUMBENT FIRM must notify the regulator and provide explanation of the reasons thereof.

Removal of incumbent auditor

4. INCUMBENT FIRM can only be removed where there are proper grounds. In case of a removal, Company and INCUMBENT FIRM must notify the regulator and provide explanation of the reasons thereof.

Appointment of INCOMING FIRM

5.   INCOMING FIRM to be appointed by the general meeting of shareholders/members.

6.   Once appointed, INCOMING FIRM to write to retiring auditor for professional clearance ('no objection' letter).

7.   INCUMBENT FIRM to obtain authorization from Company to open its prior year audit file to INCOMING FIRM.

8.   INCOMING FIRM to sign 'hold harmless' letter and to obtain access to INCUMBENT FIRM's working papers.

Russian Federation

Resignation of incumbent auditor

1.   An auditor may resign:

    (a)   if it is not the sole auditor of the company or

    (b)   at a general meeting of the company but not otherwise.

2.   If an auditor gives notice in writing to the directors of the company, the directors shall call a general meeting of the company as soon as is practicable for the purpose of appointing an auditor. On appointment of another auditor the resignation shall take effect.

Removal of incumbent auditor

3.   An auditor may be removed from office by resolution of the company at a general meeting of which special notice has been given, but not otherwise.

Appointment of INCOMING FIRM

4.   INCOMING FIRM to write to retiring auditor for professional clearance and send Company a written consent to act (included in the letter of engagement for a company statutory audit).

5.   Company directors to write to INCOMING FIRM informing INCOMING FIRM of its appointment and to INCUMBENT FIRM that their resignation has been effected.

6.   INCOMING FIRM to write to INCUMBENT FIRM requesting professional clearance and access to prior year's working papers.

7.   INCUMBENT FIRM to send professional clearance letter and grant access to prior year's working papers to INCOMING FIRM.

Spain
Specific regulations and requirements
1. Resignation or dismissal of INCUMBENT FIRM can occur in very limited situations.
Resignation of incumbent auditor
2. The resignation of INCUMBENT FIRM is initiated by the election and assignment of INCOMING FIRM for the following business year (normal change of auditor).
3. Company to inform INCUMBENT FIRM of the reason for termination of the audit engagement. INCUMBENT FIRM to inform the audit regulator.
Appointment of INCOMING FIRM
4. Company to elect INCOMING FIRM as auditor by ordinary resolution at a general assembly meeting/shareholders' meeting. According to the local audit law, the first appointment must be for three years or more, but not longer than nine years for the following business year (normal change of auditor).
5. INCOMING FIRM to ensure it has met the requirements for appointment as statutory auditor.
6. If an audit engagement audit is ended through termination for good cause by INCUMBENT FIRM or through revocation (premature change of auditor), INCOMING FIRM may only accept the engagement if it has been informed by INCUMBENT FIRM about the reason for the termination or revocation and the findings of the audit to date.

Switzerland

Proposal to appoint INCOMING FIRM

1.	Company to propose ordinary resolution for the annual general meeting 2020 to appoint INCOMING FIRM.

Company to send a copy of the special notice arising from the resolution to INCOMING FIRM.

2.	When the resolution to appoint INCOMING FIRM is passed, Company to send a note to the Register of Commerce within 14 days.

Appointment of INCOMING FIRM

3.	INCOMING FIRM to write to Company covering:

••	that our internal rules of professional conduct require us to communicate with INCUMBENT FIRM to seek information, which could influence our decision as to whether we may accept appointment;

••	that we request Company to inform INCUMBENT FIRM of the proposed change (unless it has already done this) and to give INCUMBENT FIRM authority to discuss its affairs with us.

4.	Company to give INCOMING FIRM permission to speak to INCUMBENT FIRM and vice versa.

5.	INCOMING FIRM to request INCUMBENT FIRM to inform us of any matters which could influence our decision as to whether or not we may accept appointment.

6.	Company to appoint INCOMING FIRM as auditor by ordinary resolution at a general meeting.

Ukraine
Specific regulations and requirements

1.   New stricter rules are applicable to PIE entities starting from 1 Oct 2018. PIEs being issuers of local debt or equity. Large entities also qualify as PIE if the incoming firm meet two of these criteria: revenues exceed EUR 40m, assets exceed EUR 20m, employees exceed 250 people.

PIEs are subject to long-form audit reporting. Financial statements are to be prepared under IFRS. Auditor required to report to audit committee. Management to prepare and publish management report.

Generally, Ukraine's audit rules are like EU audit rules, including restrictions on provision of non-audit services. These are applicable if local legal entity is subject to statutory audit. Company may appoint an audit firm from a large pool of local auditors included in the register.

Rotation

2.   Ten-year rule for the audit firm, with the possibility to extend for another 10 years if audit is tendered (14 years if joint audit).

3.   Seven-year rotation rule for lead audit partner.

Appointment of INCOMING FIRM

4.   The general meeting (or supervisory board) to appoint INCOMING FIRM.

Information exchange

5.   There is no legal requirement that the incumbent auditor provides working papers to INCOMING FIRM. However, if INCOMING FIRM considers a review of the working papers of the incumbent auditor will be useful, it is common practice to grant access. Both Company and the incumbent auditor to sign 'hold harmless' letters. (*INCUMBENT FIRM is not the local auditor)

United Kingdom

<u>Resignation of incumbent auditor</u>

1. INCUMBENT FIRM to deposit a section 519 statement of the circumstances connected with ceasing to hold office with Company to be brought to the attention of the members or creditors of Company.

2. Company has 14 days from the deposit of the section 519 statement to the Registrar of Companies to either circulate it to the members and to others entitled to receive copies of the accounts or apply to the court for permission not to circulate.

3. INCUMBENT FIRM must notify the FRC Professional Oversight Board of ceasing to hold office accompanied by a copy of the section 519 statement at the same time as the section 519 statement is deposited with Company.

4. INCUMBENT FIRM to deposit the section 519 statement of the circumstances connected with ceasing to hold office with the Registrar of Companies within 28 days of depositing with Company.

5. Company must notify the FRC that INCUMBENT FIRM has ceased to hold office. The notice must be accompanied by a statement of reasons and be given within 14 days after INCUMBENT FIRM's statement is deposited with Company.

6. Company to hold a general meeting to remove INCUMBENT FIRM by ordinary resolution. Company to send a copy of the special notice arising from the resolution to INCUMBENT FIRM.

7. When the resolution to remove INCUMBENT FIRM is passed, Company to send a note to the Registrar of Companies within 14 days.

Appointment of INCOMING FIRM

8.   INCOMING FIRM and INCUMBENT FIRM to obtain authorization from Company to communicate.

9.   INCOMING FIRM to request and obtain a professional clearance letter from INCUMBENT FIRM.

10.   INCOMING FIRM to confirm in writing acceptance of nomination as auditor.

11.   Directors to appoint INCOMING FIRM as auditor to fill a vacancy until the next AGM.

12.   Company to appoint INCOMING FIRM as auditor by ordinary resolution at the AGM.

13.   If registered with the Financial Conduct Authority, Company to notify the FCA of the change of auditor.

North America Latin America
Canada
Appointment of INCOMING FIRM

1. Company to alert INCOMING FIRM that the incoming firm will be proposed to the shareholders or directors as new auditor.
2. INCOMING FIRM to be appointed by shareholders or proposed by board to shareholders.
3. As soon as possible, INCOMING FIRM to send letter to INCUMBENT FIRM required under provincial rules of professional conduct.
4. INCUMBENT FIRM to send response.
5. INCOMING FIRM to send request to INCUMBENT FIRM to review prior year working papers. This letter is optional; the request could be made by Company or by phone.
6. INCUMBENT FIRM to obtain consent from Company to allow access to working papers by INCOMING FIRM. Note that this approval can be informal and can be obtained verbally or via email.
7. INCUMBENT FIRM to send release letter to INCOMING FIRM to be signed before review occurs.

United States

1.   There are no specific requirements in respect of removing or appointing auditors.

Insurance Companies

2.   Company to notify the insurance commissioner of the state of domicile of the name and address of INCUMBENT FIRM. Company obtains and files with its domiciliary state insurance commissioner an awareness letter from INCOMING FIRM.

3.   Company to notify the insurance department of the state of domicile within 5 business days of the dismissal or resignation of INCUMBENT FIRM. Within 10 business days of that notification, Company is also required to provide a letter stating whether there were any disagreements, subsequently resolved or not, within the past 24 months with INCUMBENT FIRM on any matter of accounting principles or practices including financial statement disclosure, auditing scope or procedures which, if not resolved to the satisfaction of INCUMBENT FIRM, would have caused INCUMBENT FIRM to refer to the subject matter of the disagreement in the audit opinion. Company obtains letter from INCUMBENT FIRM addressed to Company stating whether INCUMBENT FIRM agrees with the statements contained in the Company's letter and, if not, stating the reasons for INCUMBENT FIRM's disagreement. Company provides letter from INCUMBENT FIRM to the

insurance department at the same time as the Company's letter. The letter for Puerto Rico is due within 30 days of the appointment of INCOMING FIRM.

Brazil
Rotation

1. The audit partner is required to rotate after a maximum of five years (this is applicable to Company) for large entities, and after ten years for smaller entities.

Appointment of INCOMING FIRM

2. Once authorized to do so by Company, INCUMBENT FIRM to provide INCOMING FIRM access to supporting documentation and information obtained during prior year audit period (Item VI, article 25, Instruction CVM 380/99).

Chile
Specific regulations and requirements

1. Chilean Law No. 18,046, regarding stock corporations, regulates the engagement of external auditors.

    Stock corporations must appoint external auditors at the annual general meeting (Article 56 Law No. 18,046).

Rotation

2. 1) Article 243 paragraph f) Law No. 18,045 sets forth that lead audit partners shall rotate every five years.

    2) For audit clients that are not overseen by the Commission for the Financial Market, the INCOMING FIRM

    Global Independence Policy is applicable:

(a)   Public interest entities: rotation of the lead partner and Quality Review Partner should never exceed seven years.

(b)   Other entities (i.e. private entities): rotation of the lead audit partner should never exceed ten years.

Resignation of incumbent auditor

3.   An external audit firm may resign an audit engagement in accordance with professional standards and/or the respective engagement letter. Notice should be issued to the audited entity's management. If the audited entity is overseen by the CMF or other relevant regulatory agency for financial reporting purposes, the external audit firm should send a notice to such agency.

New auditor shall be appointed by the entity in accordance with applicable law and/or its by-laws. For stock corporations, an extraordinary general meeting shall be called if resignation takes place after the annual general meeting.

Removal of incumbent auditor

4.   The audited entity's management may decide to remove the auditor in accordance with the respective engagement letter and/or the applicable law. If the audited entity is overseen by the CMF or other relevant regulatory agency for financial reporting purposes, the incoming firm should send notice to such agency.

New auditor shall be appointed by the entity in accordance with applicable law and/or its by-laws.

For stock corporations, an extraordinary general meeting shall be called if the removal takes place after the annual general meeting.

Appointment of INCOMING FIRM

5.   Company to appoint INCOMING FIRM in accordance with applicable law and its by-laws. We understand that Company is a closed stock corporation and is not regulated or overseen by the CMF or other relevant regulatory agency for the purposes of its financial reporting.
6.   INCOMING FIRM to write to INCUMBENT FIRM requesting a professional clearance and access to prior year's working papers.
7.   INCUMBENT FIRM to respond with clearance letter and grant access to the working papers.

Mexico
Specific regulations and requirements

1.   Entities are required to prepare financial statements at year-end periods in compliance with MFRS for approval at the annual ordinary general shareholders' meeting by or before April 30 each year.

        Audited financial statements are not required. However, interested third parties (clients, suppliers and other interested parties) expect that significant entities are audited in accordance with International Standards on Auditing. Audited financial statements are a requirement for certain commercial bids and financing.

Rotation

2.   For non-public entities, there is no legal provision to rotate auditor.

Resignation of incumbent auditor

3.   For non-public entities, it is common practice for a change of auditor to be approved at a meeting of the

Board of Directors or general management and for the auditor to be notified of the decision.

Appointment of INCOMING FIRM

4. INCOMING FIRM to contact INCUMBENT FIRM before accepting the engagement to discuss the reasons of the change.

5. Company to hold a board of directors or general management meeting to approve the change of external auditor.

6. For non-public entities, there is no legal provision to report the change of auditor.

7. There is no legal requirement to submit the audit service proposal for non-public entities.

Panama

Appointment of INCOMING FIRM

1. Company to send a letter to INCUMBENT FIRM communicating the change of auditor.
2. Company to authorize INCOMING FIRM to review INCUMBENT FIRM's working papers.
3. Company to give INCOMING FIRM permission to speak to INCUMBENT FIRM and vice versa.

Asia-Pacific and Africa
Australia

Rotation

1.   There are no mandatory audit firm or partner rotation rules in Australia for private companies. If the entity is considered a PIE, then partner rotation is after seven years.

Resignation of incumbent auditor

2.   Company to inform INCUMBENT FIRM of intention to change auditor. This letter should be printed on the company's letterhead.

Appointment of INCOMING FIRM

3.   At the AGM Company may appoint an auditor at its AGM only if a member of the company gives written notice of the nomination 21 days before the AGM (CA s328B(1)).

Company must send a copy of the notice to the proposed nominated auditor, the current auditor, and persons entitled to receive notice of general meetings of Company.

The copy of the notice of nomination must be sent not less than 7 days before the meeting.

Outside the AGM

The nomination of appointment will be required before the incoming auditor appointment is confirmed by the members at the next AGM – see step 19 below.

4.   Company to request that INCOMING FIRM consents to act as auditor and to authorize INCOMING FIRM to

communicate with INCUMBENT FIRM. A copy of the nomination should be included.

5. INCOMING FIRM to respond to request to consent to act as auditor after checking compliance with Client Acceptance Procedures.

6. INCOMING FIRM to request ethical clearance from INCUMBENT FIRM (APES 110 Code of Ethics for professional accountants, specifically paragraphs 210.10 to 210.14)

7. INCUMBENT FIRM to provide ethical clearance to ascertain if there are any professional reasons why the appointment should not be accepted.

8. INCUMBENT FIRM to submit Form 342 to ASIC for consent of resignation.

9. INCOMING FIRM to confirm in writing to Company (with copy to INCUMBENT FIRM) that it is prepared to accept the appointment subject to ASIC's approval of resignation (This should not be provided until ethical clearance has been received) AND if the change is close to reporting deadline (more likely where resignation outside AGM), that it can conduct an effective audit before the reporting deadline.

10. Company to sign resolution appointing INCOMING FIRM subject to ASIC's approval of resignation.

11. Company to confirm in writing that:
    •• there are no disagreements between INCUMBENT FIRM and the management or directors (as defined in RG 26);
    •• there are no reasons to give an inability to complete any audit under the Corporations Act 2001 or the National Consumer Credit Protection Regulations 2010.

12. INCUMBENT FIRM to provide details on the timing of the proposed resignation and whether INCUMBENT FIRM provided an adverse or disclaimer of opinion or qualification within the two most recent financial years and any subsequent interim period. This information is provided in the Form 342.

13. ASIC consent will take effect when the following information is provided:
   •• details of INCUMBENT FIRM
   •• details of INCOMING FIRM
   •• the reason for the change of auditor.

   This is done via:
   •• for listed disclosing entities – given to ASIC and any relevant market operator via a continuous disclosure notice (which would not deal with other matters);
   •• for unlisted disclosing entities – notify ASIC using Form 1003 Disclosure notice for unlisted disclosing entity;
   •• for non-disclosing public entities – company to provide the information via public notice on company website, by email or in writing.

   ASIC Regulatory Guide 26 provides more information on the above.

14. INCOMING FIRM to provide formal consent to act as auditor subject to appointment at the next AGM/directors' meeting, once ASIC consent of the resignation of the outgoing auditor is obtained.

15. INCUMBENT FIRM to give formal notice of resignation after the receipt of ASIC consent to resignation.

16. Company to submit Form 315 (notification of resignation of auditor) to ASIC within 14 days of receiving INCUMBENT FIRM resignation.
17. Company to write to INCOMING FIRM confirming appointment as auditor.
18. INCOMING FIRM to issue engagement letter.
19. Directors to appoint INCOMING FIRM to hold office only until the next AGM. The appointment must then be confirmed by the members following the procedures set out below.
20. Written notice of notification

Company may appoint an auditor only at its AGM (and reappoint when the auditor was appointed by the directors during the year) if a member of the company gives the company written notice of the nomination 21 days before the AGM (CA s328B (1)).

Company must send a copy of the notice to INCOMING FIRM, INCUMBENT FIRM, and persons entitled to receive notice of general meetings of Company.

The copy of the notice of nomination must be sent not less than 7 days before the meeting.

The notice of the nomination for appointment as auditor can be combined with the notice of the AGM where appropriate.

21. Notice of AGM

A meeting of members of Company (including an AGM) must be convened giving at least 21 days (28 days for listed companies) notice, or such longer period as is specified in Company's constitution (CA ss249H, 249HA). A copy of the notice of the meeting, and of any other communications relating to the meeting that a member is entitled to receive, must be sent to INCUMBENT FIRM (CA s249K).

China

Resignation by auditor before end of term of office

1. INCUMBENT FIRM to issue a letter of resignation to Company.
2. Company to hold a board of directors meeting to accept the resignation of INCUMBENT FIRM.

Appointment of INCOMING FIRM

3. Depending on the provisions of the Articles of Association, the general manager or CFO or a meeting of the board of directors to appoint INCOMING FIRM.
4. After the appointment, INCOMING FIRM to obtain Company authorization letter to communicate with INCUMBENT FIRM.
5. INCOMING FIRM to issue letter to INCUMBENT FIRM to enquire on ethical matters, significant accounting or auditing issues, fraud, non-compliance, control of material weaknesses, and other matters which could influence the decision as to whether to accept appointment.
6. INCUMBENT FIRM to issue professional clearance letter to INCOMING FIRM.

Hong Kong

Resignation by auditor before end of term of office

1. Company to remove INCUMBENT FIRM by ordinary resolution at a general meeting which requires special notice i.e. 28-day notice. Company to send a copy of the special notice to INCUMBENT FIRM.
2. Company must deliver a notice to the Registrar for registration within 15 days beginning on the date on which the special resolution is passed.
3. INCUMBENT FIRM to submit 'Letter of Resignation or Termination' to the board of directors and audit committee.
4. INCUMBENT FIRM to provide statement to Company at least 14 days before the end of the appointment period or within 14 days beginning on the date of termination. The statement should detail whether there are circumstances that should be brought to the attention of Company's members and creditors.
5. Within 21 days beginning on the date on which Company receives the statement, INCUMBENT FIRM must deliver a copy of the statement to the Registrar for registration within the next 7 days.
6. Within 14 days beginning on the date on which it receives the 'Statement of Circumstances', Company to send out a copy of the statement to every member of Company or apply to the court, not this statement.
7. INCUMBENT FIRM may make representation in writing to Company and request notification to members of Company. Company to send the

representation of INCUMBENT FIRM/give notice to members before the meeting.

8. Additional procedures are applicable to a Hong Kong-licensed corporation, or an associated entity of a HK-licensed corporation or registered institution.

9. Company must send a copy of the resolution to both INCOMING FIRM and INCUMBENT FIRM.

Appointment of INCOMING FIRM

10. Company to appoint INCOMING FIRM by a resolution passed at the AGM held in respect of the previous financial year and copies of written resolution for appointment must be sent to INCOMING FIRM and INCUMBENT FIRM.

11. INCOMING FIRM to write to Company to request permission to communicate with INCUMBENT FIRM to enquire whether there is any professional or other reason for the proposed change of which INCOMING FIRM ought to be aware.

12. Company to give INCOMING FIRM permission to communicate with INCUMBENT FIRM.

India

Removal of auditor before end of term of office

1. Company to hold meeting of the board of directors to pass a resolution to remove the incumbent auditor.
2. Before taking any action Company must give the auditor reasonable opportunity to be heard.
3. The application for removal of auditor shall be made in Form ADT-2 within 30 days of resolution passed by the board.
4. Company to hold a general meeting within 60 days from the date of approval to remove for auditor to pass of the special resolution.

Appointment of INCOMING FIRM for statutory reporting

5. Audit committee to recommend INCOMING FIRM as statutory auditor to the board of directors to recommend to the annual general meeting for appointment.
6. Directors to obtain written consent from INCOMING FIRM to such appointment, and a certificate of eligibility for such appointment under the Companies Act, 2013.
7. For a listed company, notice to shareholders for an annual general meeting shall include proposed fee and basis for recommendation for appointment.
8. The shareholders to appoint INCOMING FIRM at the annual general meeting.
9. Company to inform INCOMING FIRM of its appointment and file a notice of such appointment in

form ADT 1 with the Registrar of Companies within 15 days of appointment.

Note: The appointment of auditor is for five years and can continue for a maximum two terms of five years each for:

•• all listed companies
•• all unlisted public companies with paid-up share capital of Rs 10 crore or more
•• all private limited companies with paid-up share capital of Rs 50 crore or more
•• all companies with public borrowings from financial institutions, banks or public deposits of Rs 50 crore or more irrespective of paid-up share capital.

10. INCOMING FIRM to issue letter to the incumbent auditor to enquire about professional or other reasons why it should not accept the appointment.

11. Incumbent auditor to issue professional clearance letter to INCUMBENT FIRM.

12. INCOMING FIRM to sign engagement letter.

Rotation of signing partner, governed by INCOMING FIRM policies

13. Audit partner to rotate after seven years for all listed companies.

Appointment of INCOMING FIRM for group reporting

14. If appointment is only for reporting on group packs, then appointment under Companies Act 2013 is not required.

Note: For the purpose of holding board meetings/general meetings of shareholders Company will need to follow due process as prescribed under the Companies Act, 2013.

Indonesia

Specific regulations and requirements

1. There are no specific regulations and requirements regarding the resignation and appointment of external auditor. However, we consider the following:
   - Limited Company Law No. 40/2007.
   - Public Accountant Law No. 5/2011.
   - Ministry of Finance Regulation No. 154/PMK.01/2017.
   - Indonesian Auditing Standard.

Rotation

2. No mandatory firm rotation.

Ten-year rule for all audit partners with two-year cooling-off period.

Resignation of incumbent auditor

3. As mentioned above, no specific regulations or requirements apply.

Appointment of INCOMING FIRM

4. INCOMING FIRM should not accept appointment until communications with INCUMBENT FIRM have been evaluated.
5. INCOMING FIRM to write to INCUMBENT FIRM requesting a professional objection letter and access to prior year's working papers.

6.   INCUMBENT FIRM to respond to professional objection letter and grant access to prior year's working papers.

Ivory Coast/Cote d'Ivoire

Specific regulations and requirements

1. Statutory auditors are appointed by the shareholders for a six-year term (Refer to Art 704 to Uniform act relating to commercial companies and economic interest group). The statutory auditor cannot be dismissed before the end of the period of appointment. Resignation can occur in very limited situations. The same rules apply to the substitute statutory auditor, which is appointed at the same time as the statutory auditor.

Resignation of incumbent auditor

2. INCUMBENT FIRM cannot resign except for specific legitimate reasons provided by the Code of Ethics. The following shall constitute a legitimate reason to resign:
    (a)   The definitive discontinuance of business
    (b)   Pressing personal reasons, on the grounds of health
    (c)   Difficulties encountered in carrying out the engagement which are impossible to resolve
    (d)   The occurrence of an event that may compromise compliance with professional standards and impair the independence or objectivity of the statutory auditor.
3. Where, at the expiry of the mandate of INCUMBENT FIRM, it is proposed to the meeting of shareholders not to renew INCUMBENT FIRM's mandate,

INCUMBENT FIRM may, at their request, be heard by the meeting of shareholders.

4. INCOMING FIRM to send an acceptance letter prior to the shareholders' meeting.

5. The shareholders to appoint INCOMING FIRM by the proposal of the Board of Directors.

6. Company to send to INCOMING FIRM the minutes of the shareholders' meeting and the declaration and acknowledgement of the auditor. Company to publish the nomination.

7. INCOMING FIRM to write to INCUMBENT FIRM to obtain access to working papers.

Japan

Specific regulations and requirements

1. The following companies shall have a statutory auditor:
    (a) A stock company which has an audit and supervisory committee
    (b) A stock company which has a nominating committee, an audit committee and a compensation committee
    (c) A stock company that satisfies any of the following requirements:
        (i) The stated capital in the balance sheet as of the end of its most recent business year is 500 million yen or more.
        (ii) The total sum in the liabilities section of the balance sheet as of the end of its most recent business year is 20 billion yen or more.

    Other stock companies may have a statutory auditor as prescribed by the articles of incorporation.
2. A statutory auditor is appointed by a resolution at a shareholders' meeting for a one-year term.

<u>Resignation of incumbent auditor</u>

3. INCUMBENT FIRM is appointed for a one-year period and changed when the term ends (i.e. resignation during the term is very limited).

4. Notwithstanding the above, INCUMBENT FIRM may be dismissed at any time by a resolution at a shareholders' meeting. Also, Company/the company auditor (*) may dismiss INCUMBENT FIRM if INCUMBENT FIRM:

    a) has breached the obligations in the course of duty, or neglected the financial auditor's duties

    b) has engaged in misconduct inappropriate for a financial auditor

    c) has difficulty in, or is unable to cope with the execution of the financial auditor's duties due to mental or physical disability.

    (*) where applicable, the company auditor should be read as board of company auditors, audit and supervisory committee, or an audit committee.

<u>Appointment of INCOMING FIRM</u>

5. Company and INCOMING FIRM to exchange non-disclosure agreement so the company can provide information necessary for INCOMING FIRM to decide whether to accept the appointment and to make a proposal.

6. Company, including the company auditor (*), to decide internally on the statutory auditor change.

7. Company to notify INCOMING FIRM and INCUMBENT FIRM of the auditor change.

8. INCOMING FIRM to contact the statutory auditor to obtain certain information as part of the acceptance procedures required by audit standards.

9. The company auditor (*) to determine content of proposals to be submitted to the shareholders' meeting, regarding election of INCOMING FIRM and dismissal of or refusal to re-elect INCUMBENT FIRM.

10. Company to make a resolution at the shareholders' meeting to appoint INCOMING FIRM as the new statutory auditor.

11. Company to register the change in statutory auditor within two weeks following the shareholders' meeting resolution.

Malaysia

Resignation of incumbent auditor

1. Company to notify INCUMBENT FIRM and INCOMING FIRM of intention to change auditor.
2. INCUMBENT FIRM to give notice of resignation as auditor.

Appointment of INCOMING FIRM

3. INCOMING FIRM to seek professional clearance from INCUMBENT FIRM in accordance with the by-laws of the Malaysian Institute of Accountants.
4. Once professional clearance is obtained from INCUMBENT FIRM, INCOMING FIRM to issue a letter of consent to Company to act as statutory auditor of Company.
5. Company to convene a general meeting (normally at the annual general meeting) to obtain approval on the change of auditor.
6. INCOMING FIRM to be re-appointed for each financial year.

New Zealand

Retirement of incumbent auditor/Resignation by auditor before end of term of office

1. Company to send INCUMBENT FIRM a letter requesting resignation (INCOMING FIRM copied on this letter).
2. Company to obtain INCUMBENT FIRM's letter of resignation.
3. Company to provide INCOMING FIRM a letter to request INCOMING FIRM to fill a casual vacancy or accept nomination as auditor.

Appointment of INCOMING FIRM

4. INCOMING FIRM to write to INCUMBENT FIRM requesting professional clearance and access to audit files.
5. INCOMING FIRM to obtain professional clearance letter from INCUMBENT FIRM to confirm that no professional reasons exist why INCOMING FIRM should not accept appointment as auditor of Company.
6. INCOMING FIRM to write to Company to accept appointment/nomination as auditor.

Nigeria

Retirement of incumbent auditor/Resignation by auditor before end of term of office

1.   INCUMBENT FIRM may resign office by depositing a notice in writing to that effect at Company's registered office.
2.   The notice shall be sent to the Commission and members of Company within 14 days of receipt.
This requirement may be set aside by court order.
3.   INCUMBENT FIRM may request Company to convene an extraordinary general meeting for explanation of the circumstances of their resignation.
4.   Company is required to convene a meeting (within 21 days from the date of the deposit of a requisition) for a day not more than 28 days after the date on which the notice convening the meeting is given. This requirement may be set aside by court order.

Appointment of INCOMING FIRM

5.   Company to appoint INCOMING FIRM at each annual general meeting; this is automatic for a retiring auditor except upon disqualification, removal or resignation.
6.   Directors may appoint a person to fill the vacancy where no auditors are appointed or reappointed.
7.   Directors shall inform the commission within a week where the INCOMING FIRM exercise their powers as above.
8.   Company may replace INCUMBENT FIRM (at an AGM) with INCOMING FIRM nominated by a member

once a 14- day nomination notice has been given to members.

9. Company to inform INCUMBENT FIRM of the proposed change, permit professional enquiry from INCOMING FIRM about client matters and ensure INCUMBENT FIRM has validly vacated office.

10. INCOMING FIRM to write to INCUMBENT FIRM seeking information which could influence the decision to accept the engagement and decline appointment if Company refuses INCUMBENT FIRM permission to discuss company matters.

Pakistan

<u>Specific regulations and requirements</u>

1. As per section 246 (2) of Companies Act, 2017:
    "............... the subsequent auditor or auditors shall be appointed by the company in the annual general meeting on the recommendation of the board after obtaining consent of the proposed auditors, a notice shall be given to the members with the notice of general meeting. The auditor or auditors so appointed shall retire on the conclusion of the next annual general meeting."
    For local appointment compliance, INCOMING FIRM Pakistan to provide consent on prescribed format to Company at least seven days before the Board meeting for appointment of auditor. This will be done post-appointment of INCOMING FIRM globally and must be initiated by Company, i.e. seeking INCOMING FIRM Pakistan's consent to act as auditor.

<u>Rotation</u>

2. As per Regulation 34 of Listed Companies (Code of Corporate Governance) Regulations, 2017:
    (1) All listed companies in the financial sector shall change their external auditor every five years.
    (2) All listed companies other than those in the financial sector shall, at the minimum, rotate the engagement partner every five years.

Resignation of incumbent auditor

3.   If INCUMBENT FIRM has been changed after the expiry of its term of appointment of one year from last AGM to next AGM, there is no specific legal requirement for resignation of INCUMBENT FIRM.

Appointment of INCOMING FIRM

4.   As per Regulation 33 (3) of Listed Companies (Code of Corporate Governance) Regulations, 2017: INCOMING FIRM to contact INCUMBENT FIRM for professional clearance. If such response/clearance cannot be obtained before providing consent on the prescribed format, then such consent is made subject to receipt of clearance from INCUMBENT FIRM.

Philippines

Rotation

1. For non-public companies, INCOMING FIRM rotation policy applies wherein engagement leaders must rotate after ten years or seven years.

Resignation of incumbent auditor

2. The auditor is elected every year by the board of directors upon proposal of management or the audit committee.

Appointment of INCOMING FIRM

3. Company's board of directors to approve appointment of INCOMING FIRM.
4. Company to enter into engagement with INCOMING FIRM.
5. Company to advise INCUMBENT FIRM of the change and request INCUMBENT FIRM to allow INCOMING FIRM to review prior year working papers.
6. INCUMBENT FIRM to issue a "hold harmless" letter for INCOMING FIRM to sign prior to review of working papers.
7. INCOMING FIRM to review prior year working papers.

Singapore

Rotation

1.   Non-PIE engagement partner: 10 years.
No rotation rules for audit firms.

Resignation of incumbent auditor

2.   Non-public interest company
205AA. – (1) An auditor of a non-public interest company (other than a company which is subsidiary company of a public interest company) may resign before the end of the term of office by giving the company notice of resignation.

(2)   Where a notice of resignation is given under subsection (1), the auditor's term of office expires:

(a)   at the end of the day on which notice is given to the company; or

(b)   if notice specifies a time on a later day for the purpose, at that time.

Within 14 days beginning on the date on which a company receives a notice of resignation under subsection (1), the company must lodge with the Registrar a notification of that fact in such form as the Registrar may require.

3.   Public interest company or subsidiary company of public interest company
205AB – (1) An auditor of a public interest company, or a subsidiary company of a public interest company,

may by giving the company a notice of resignation in writing, resign before the end of the term of office for which the auditor or subsidiary company was appointed, if:

(a) the auditor has applied for consent from the Registrar to the resignation and provided a written statement of reasons for resignation and, at or about the same time as the application, notified the company in writing of the application to the Registrar and provided the company with the written statement of reasons for resignation; and

(b) the consent of the Registrar has been given.

(1) The registrar shall, as soon as practicable after receiving the application from an auditor under subsection (1), notify the auditor and the company whether it consents to the resignation of the auditor.

(2) A statement made by an auditor in an application to the Registrar under subsection (1)(a) or in answer to an enquiry by the Registrar relating to the reasons for the application:

(a) is not admissible in evidence in any civil or criminal proceedings against the auditor; and

(b) subject to subsection (4), may not be made the grounds for a prosecution, an action or a suit against the auditor, and a certificate by the Registrar that the statement was made in the application or in the answer to the enquiry by the registrar is conclusive evidence that the statement was so made.

4. Written statement to be disseminated unless application to court made 205AC – (1) Where an auditor of a public interest company, or a subsidiary company of a public interest company, gives the company a notice of resignation under section 205AB,

the company must within 14 days after receiving the notice of resignation and the written statement of the auditor's reasons for resignation (referred to in this section and sections 205AD and 205AE as the written statement) send a copy of the written statement to every member of the company.

(2)   Copies of the written statement need not be sent out if an application is made to the court within 14 days, beginning on the date on which the company received the written statement, by either the company or any other person who claims to be aggrieved by the written statement, for determination that the auditor has abused the use of the written statement or is using the provisions of this section to secure needless publicity for defamatory matter.

(3)   In the case where an application is made under subsection (2) by:

    (a)   the company, the company must give notice of the application to the auditor of the company,

    or

    (b)   any other person, that person must give notice of the application to the company and the auditor of the company.

Appointment of INCOMING FIRM

5.   Appointment of new auditor in place of resigning auditor 205AF – (1) subject to subsection (3), if:

an auditor of a non-public company (other than a subsidiary company of a public interest company) gives notice of resignation under section 205AA (1); or an auditor of a public interest company, or a subsidiary company of a public listed company gives notice of resignation under section 205AB (1), and the registrar approves the resignation of the auditor under section 205AB (2).

The directors of the company in question:

(1)   shall call a general meeting of the company as soon as practicable, and in any case not more than 3 months after the date of the auditor's resignation, for the purpose of appointing an auditor in place of the auditor who desires to resign or has resigned; and

(2)   upon appointment of the new auditor, shall lodge with the registrar a notification of such appointment within 14 days of the appointment.

If the directors of a company fail to appoint an auditor in place of the auditor who desires to resign or has resigned, the registrar may on the application in writing of any member of the company make the appointment.

6.   Company to write to INCOMING FIRM informing us of their interest in our appointment and to INCUMBENT FIRM informing them that their resignation has been affected.

7.   INCOMING FIRM to obtain professional clearance from INCUMBENT FIRM.

8.   INCOMING FIRM to issue consent to act and letter of engagement to Company after professional clearance is obtained.

Sri Lanka

<u>Resignation of incumbent auditor</u>

1.   An auditor may resign:
     ••   if not the sole auditor of the company
     ••   at a general meeting of the company
     but not otherwise.
2.   If an auditor gives notice in writing to the directors of the company, the directors shall call a general meeting of the company as soon as is practicable for the purpose of appointing an auditor and on the appointment of another auditor the resignation shall take effect.

<u>Removal of incumbent auditor</u>

3.   An auditor of a company may be removed from office by resolution of the company at a general meeting of which special notice has been given, but not otherwise.
4.   A company shall not appoint a new auditor in place of an auditor who is qualified for re-appointment, unless:
     (a)   at least 20 working days' written notice of a proposal to do so has been given to the auditor;
     and
     (b)   the auditor has been given reasonable opportunity to make representations to the

shareholders on the appointment of another person, either in writing or by the auditor or representative at a shareholder meeting.

5. If an auditor resigns or ceases for any other reason to hold office, the auditor shall deliver to the company a statement of any circumstances which should be brought to the attention of the shareholders or creditors of the company, or a statement that there are none.

(a)   If he resigns, with the notice of resignation;

(b)   If he gives notice that he does not wish to be reappointed, with that notice;

(c)   If he ceases to hold office for any other reason, within ten working days of ceasing to hold office.

6. If the auditor has stated circumstances to be brought to the attention of the shareholders or creditors, the company shall:

(a)   send a copy of the statement to each shareholder; and

(b)   deliver a copy of the statement to the Registrar.

7. A company shall, immediately after the removal of an auditor from office give notice in writing of the removal to the Registrar and, if the company does not appoint another auditor under subsection (7), the Registrar shall appoint an auditor.

8. An auditor appointed in pursuance shall hold office until the conclusion of the next annual general meeting of the company.

Appointment of INCOMING FIRM

9. INCOMING FIRM to write to retiring auditor for professional clearance and to send the company a written consent to act (included in the letter of engagement for a company statutory audit).

10. Company to apply to the regulator for approval in appointing INCOMING FIRM as auditor.

11. Company to send at least seven days before a copy of the notice of nomination and notice of AGM/EGM to:
    •• Shareholders.
    •• INCOMING FIRM.
    •• At the EGM a resolution is passed to appoint INCOMING FIRM as auditor, and the resignation of INCUMBENT FIRM takes effect.

12. Company to write to INCOMING FIRM informing us of our appointment and to incumbent auditor informing them that their resignation has been affected.

13. INCOMING FIRM to write to INCUMBENT FIRM requesting professional clearance and access to prior year's working papers.

14. INCUMBENT FIRM to send professional clearance letter and grant access to prior year's working papers.

Additional requirement where company is listed on the Colombo Stock Exchange

15.   Company to incorporate a notice to shareholders of the proposed change as follows:

    ••   Confirmation from INCUMBENT FIRM whether the INCOMING FIRM are aware of any professional reasons why INCOMING FIRM should not accept appointment as auditor. If so, to provide details.

Thailand

Specific regulations and requirements

1. In accordance with Thai Civil and Commercial Code Section 1197, the financial statements must be examined by auditors and submitted to a general meeting for adoption within four months from the date of statement of financial position.

Rotation

2. For non-public interest entities, maximum period is 10 years.

Resignation of Incumbent auditor

3. If the resignation is at Company's request and INCUMBENT FIRM receives the formal letter from Company, INCOMING FIRM does not need to send a formal written statement to Company.

Appointment of INCOMING FIRM

4. INCOMING FIRM to obtain professional clearance from INCUMBENT FIRM.
5. Company to resolve that INCOMING FIRM is appointed as auditor at annual general meeting of shareholders.
6. INCOMING FIRM to write to INCUMBENT FIRM requesting access to prior year's working papers.
7. INCUMBENT FIRM to send professional clearance letter and grant access to prior year's working papers.

United Arab Emirates

Appointment of INCOMING FIRM

1. Company to approve the appointment of INCOMING FIRM every year (applicable for LLC companies).
2. Company (FZE or FZCO company) must not appoint an auditor who has a conflict of interest or is not independent from Company (FZE or FZCO company).
3. The shareholders may by any ordinary resolution appoint INCOMING FIRM to hold office until the close of next general meeting (for FZE and FZCO companies).
4. Company to write to INCOMING FIRM confirming appointment and to INCUMBENT FIRM confirming their resignation has been effected (applicable for all companies).
5. INCOMING FIRM to write to INCUMBENT FIRM requesting professional clearance and access to prior year's working papers (applicable for all companies).
6. INCUMBENT FIRM to send professional clearance letter and grant access to prior year's working papers (applicable for all companies).

Whilst not comprehensive, the above identifies some of the local considerations you should be mindful of in planning your transition. Its inclusion in the written proposal is yet another indication of the firm's understanding of your audit landscape and the regulatory hurdles which will need to be overcome and satisfied.

Selection Process

The arrival of the selection process does not mark the end of your journey, but it does perhaps mark the beginning of the end.

All firms will be anxious to impress your selection panel and will bring their best people to their session. It was particularly helpful when firms complimented their proposed Leadership teams by bringing to the first-round presentation other members of the team from around the world. Indeed, two firms took this to another level by bringing senior or even junior managers who would work at the sharp end of the engagement and giving them voice to express their own particular passion for working on the company audit.

In the case of the tender I managed, we split the selection process into two oral presentations. The first-round selection panel comprised the chair of the audit committee, senior management and a selection of those who would actively work closely with the appointed firm, plus the PM. All four firms were allocated two hours each to present. The firms were free to define both the content and the vehicle to be used for their presentation (power point, electronic interactive format and iPads etc.).

The intent of the first round was to identify two firms to be shortlisted to present to the final selection panel which in our case was the Group Audit Committee. Some members of management who participated in the first round were also asked to attend in order to provide their perspective and assist in addressing any points raised by the audit committee where operational matters were identified during the discussions.

The first round typically focused on each firm's proposed approach to the audit and how they differed from the current one. Audit innovation was a key opportunity, delivering both cost efficiencies and, potentially of even greater importance, a measurable reduction in the effort placed on the business at a local level in supporting the audit. This was partially driven by the fact that the company was in an advanced stage of moving significant back office functionality above market to both internal and external shared service sites. This alone provided a unique opportunity to substantially change the audit landscape and in doing so completely re-engineer our audit.

Interestingly, not all firms were ready to meet this opportunity and thus failed to communicate a vision which would work in tandem with the business as we evolved. Indeed, in many respects the message was, "Why change what works?"

Conversely, other firms worked under the mantra "what you have is good, but what you could have will be so much better".

Whilst a decision to put your audit out to tender may have been driven by the requirement of local legislation or indeed shareholder pressure, your success factors will perhaps indicate you are looking for a fresh innovative audit. It is this potential that each firm needs to understand and expand on during all touch points in your process, especially during the oral presentation when you will want to strike a chord with the audience and leave them wanting more.

The oral presentations will be an opportunity to put each firm's proposal under the spotlight; both selection panels will attempt to ensure any offered new approach will deliver tangible benefits to the business (both financial and operational) at the cost of minimal disruption.

All firms will naturally claim that they offer the best solution. One way of gaining some insight as to the legitimacy of the claims is to seek feedback from the CFOs of other companies who have transitioned their audit to the competing firms in recent years.

All attendees to both selection panels should make time to read the written proposals prior to the oral presentations. As PM I provided a written summary of the proposals along with the feedback from the fieldwork of the process to compensate for those panel members unable to dive deep into the written proposals. This, it was hoped, would ensure a meaningful discussion and focused Q&A.

I personally attended and actively participated in both rounds of the oral presentations; through these I learnt a lot about the relative merits of each firm and the proposed Lead Partners and their teams.

Following the first-round presentation by all four firms a simple questionnaire, based on the five key success factors was completed by all members of the panel, with each question being scored within the range of 1 to 5.

Following completion of this questionnaire the PM consolidated the scores and provided the outcome to the selection panel. The panel further discussed the relative merits of each firm. In the case of the tender I ran, one firm scored significantly higher than the other three, whilst two of the firms were extremely close in the middle order.

Accordingly, much of the discussion was around the differentiation of these two firms, where their audit approach differed and of even greater importance, which of the two proposed leadership teams demonstrated the best fit with the company management and its ethos.

Having arrived at the decision of which two firms should be shortlisted and invited to present to the Audit Committee in the second round, communicating the outcome was difficult and, of course, left two firms disappointed and wondering what they could have done differently.

In order to ensure that the members of the second-round selection panel were fully briefed on the feedback from the wider business and understood the outcome of the first round, along with the rationale of that decision, the PM prepared a short presentation with the charts showing the output from the various feedback assessments plus the output from the first-round questionnaire.

These charts were then adapted to provide feedback to the unsuccessful firms, with the identity of the other firms redacted. These slides also included the specific comments received relative to that firm as well as the comments from the selection panel. This feedback to all firms is a fair reflection of the investment made by them in participating in the process and as I often said to them, "Feedback is a gift; you can use it or lose it."

Obviously, all firms will wish to do everything possible to be successful and the feedback will hopefully help them hone their game towards future endeavors.

The second-round presentations were restricted to the Lead and Second signing Partners from each of the two shortlisted firms, with each firm having one hour to present. The sessions were less presentational and more a general discussion and Q&A; each firm tried to introduce a high-level overview of how an audit under their leadership would bring benefits to the company.

MHC Group Audit Tender First Round Oral Presentations selection
Please indicate your score for each firm by key success factor on the

	Firm A	Firm B	Firm C	Firm D
Proposed Lead Partner and team fit with MHC, colaborative mindset and strength of leadership along with their Experience of our Industry				
Approach to Audit Quality and the Governance within which the audit would be delivered along with reputation of the firm				
Innovation and forward thinking of the future Audit approach, leveraging Data Analytics and other opportunities for automation to deliver efficiencies particularly with regards to our evolving E2E environment and above market moves				
Value Added Services which will assist MHC in improving its control environment and in general support the evolution of our E2E initiatives				
Others indicators incl approach to Scope of the Group Audit and ensuring timely delivery of the Statutory Requirements of all 430 Statutory entities. Also the competitive Pricing of the audit engagement				

Following the second-round presentations the panel discussed with those in attendance any open points they sought clarification on before retiring to discuss which firm they recommended to the Formal Audit Committee and subsequently to the full Board before a resolution is put before shareholders at the AGM.

You might ask, with some justification, why the second-round panel which comprised the members of the Audit Committee, CEO and Group Chairman with the CFO, Head of Accounting and Reporting and the PM in attendance, did not make the recommendation. Here we move back into the depths of due Governance.

By convention and likely as defined in your Audit Committee Charter, it is the AC who have absolute accountability for ensuring delivery of a robust, compliant and independent audit report in support of your published financial statements.

Accordingly, whilst your tender process should embrace the wider business stakeholders and the final selection should be fully cognizant of their views, it is for the AC to collectively arrive at its own considered recommendation.

The formal Audit Committee will then minute its recommendation and provide the Board with its rationale in seeking its support. In most cases the Board will accept the recommendation and it will then be for the shareholders to ratify this at the AGM.

Transition Planning

The on-boarding of your newly appointed audit firm will be a complex and resource-intensive exercise. The planning of it is key and will also be heavily reliant on the engagement and goodwill of your incumbent audit firm. Ideally, you will have a window of 15 to 18 months to effect the transition, although I am aware of cases where this was only three months. I can only imagine the pressure on the organization that this short window represented.

As outlined in the section covering the Written Proposal (Chapter 13) some firms will provide both a high-level transition plan and a detailed list of transition issues impacting all key markets. The PM needs to expand on this to include the impacts and touch points for the company's finance community.

In my own case I was able to draw on the experience of the new firm in transitioning, although, of course, in all probability all the "big four" would have offered similar expertise, given the prevalence of auditor rotation.

Planning for the transition should be a team effort. Logically, the PM who managed the tender will be best placed to also oversee the transition, given that he/she has worked closely with the firm during the tender, understands better than most what the defining points were that gave rise to their success as well as knowing the personalities and internal dynamics of those involved. The firm should also allocate transition responsibility to a senior member of their team.

In defining the transition project, I identified four key areas of focus within which the company would allocate resources.

These were:

1.   Central (Both Central Accounting and Financial Reporting Consolidation)
2.   Above Market (including all internal and external shared service providers)
3.   Markets (Both material Group scope markets and statutory audit markets)
4.   IT/ Data Analytics

Each focus area (work stream) was asked to nominate both a team lead and key team members who would allocate a minimum of 50% of their time to the transition. Similarly, the firm mirrored this structure and added further to it for work streams less relevant to the company and more to the on-boarding of their own teams. As PM I coordinated activities whilst leaving the stream leads to manage matters reporting to the project coordination team on a bi-weekly basis.

To ensure adequate resources were available to each work stream and that there was good interaction within these teams and their audit firm counterpart, a project steering committee was established who met monthly to facilitate regular feedback from each work stream and ensure all deliverables were met.

The close interaction with the incumbent firm was essential. To this end a round table meeting soon after the decision was announced is key. Whilst this may be an awkward meeting for all parties, it is important that both firms accept the decision and work together in an open and collaborative manner.

The need for work shadowing and sharing of working papers, both for the transition period and prior year is essential to facilitate delivering a seamless transition. The ways of working between the firms during the transition is for the firms collectively to agree. Logic says this should not be an issue as there is every possibility that in other engagements a transition situation in the other direction could occur, so it is in both of their interests to work in a collaborative fashion.

The PM should be available to help facilitate information sharing between the incumbent and the new firm and in doing so ensure appropriate approvals are provided by the company to enable file sharing in a timely manner.

The transition is both a period during which the new firm will build on its understanding of all that the audit entails and the complexities and specifics of risk that will require close attention and also the time for them to get closer to all the operational markets. Obviously, during the tender process, it has not been possible to expose them and their local teams to all markets, if for no other reason than time constraints. Therefore, whilst the firm will have visited key markets and locations during the tender, the transition period is essential in on-boarding all teams around the world. This, where possible, should also enable members of the Leadership team to join these meetings either in person or via skype/teams.

In my case very soon after the announcement I was inundated with requests from the markets to meet with the firm's local representatives, so it was important that I established a wider visit agenda and communicated this to all stakeholders.

Today I am beginning the planning for the transition in earnest. This will inevitably become yet another journey of discovery and likely the subject of yet another book, but for now I will leave its contents to another day.

If you are embarking on an audit tender, I wish you well, stay focused and enjoy your journey.

About The Author

In 2018, Graham Hall was appointed Global Finance Project Manager charged with defining and managing a Global Audit Tender Process for one of Europe's most valuable companies with operations in over 180 countries.

He has thus experienced first-hand the full end-to-end process from the decision to tender through the set-up of the tender process, the tender, the decision and subsequent transition of auditors.

The decision to tender an audit is a complex and a troubling one for many companies owing to the high level of change being experienced already within the organization.

The 2020 COVID-19 pandemic added further to the stress already faced by many companies.

During his experience of this decision process he often heard management exchange counter views, for example, "We are going through so much change as an organization; this is not the time to be contemplating a change in auditor." Conversely, "It is because we are going through so much change that now is the time to change auditor."

An audit tender is best described as a true journey of discovery. This certainly applies to the firms and their people working on the pursuit, but also for many people working for the company, who have had little experience of what the other firms could bring to an audit and have created a close affinity and comfort with the incumbent firm.

Having taken the decision to move ahead with a tender, it is crucial to ensure a strong project manager is appointed. This person needs extensive knowledge of the business and a reasonably high profile across its finance community in order to ensure all aspects of the business engage and collaborate with the process.

From the perspective of companies, when he was first tasked with defining a process, the logical place to look was online for some true, practical guidance and maybe some firsthand experiences; he came away largely empty handed.

Yes, there are some high level "things to do" but reality bites, and what was missing was a "sounding board" with proven experience of the potholes he would encounter once he embarked on the journey.

Having completed the tender, he decided to put down on paper all the things he learnt and the experiences he had during the process. This book is his attempt to document an audit tender process in the hope that his own particular journey of discovery will resonate with the reader and maybe even help them as they too commence a similar journey.

Author Acknowledgements

I would like to acknowledge the opportunity I was afforded in being asked to manage the audit tender. The company and its management around the world were both supportive and fully engaged in the process I defined, ensuring my own journey of discovery was both exciting and fruitful.

Of course, an audit tender would not be complete without the active participation of the audit firms. I would like to sincerely thank all the Partners and staff of the "Big Four" audit firms who engaged with passion and professionalism to the tender. I know only one firm ended the process successful, but to my mind you were all winners.

Publisher Acknowledgements

The publisher would like to thank Russell Spencer, Matt Vidler, Laura-Jayne Humphrey, Lianne Bailey-Woodward, Leonard West, Edward Winters and Susan Woodard for their hard work and efforts to bring this book to publication.

The publisher would also like to thank Ben Lupton for their excellent cover design and of course the author Graham Hall for allowing them to publish this book.

About The Publisher

LR Price Publications is dedicated to publishing books by unknown authors.

We use a mixture of traditional and modern publishing methods to bring our authors' words to the wider world.

We print, publish, distribute and market books in a variety of formats including paper and hard back, electronic books e-books, digital audio books and online.

If you are an author interested in getting your book published; or a book retailer interested in selling our books, please contact us.

www.lrpricepublications.com
L.R. Price Publications Ltd,
27 Old Gloucester Street,
London, WC1N 3AX.
(0203) 051 9572
publishing@lrprice.com